A Policeman's Story
Paul Thompson

Media Enterprises Ltd
2013

CIP

The College of The Bahamas Libraries and Instructional Media Services
Cataloguing-in-Publication Data

Thompson, Paul.
A policeman's story / Paul Thompson.
p. cm.

ISBN 978-976-8231-18-5

1. Police--Bahamas--Biography. 2. Criminal investigation--Bahamas--History. 3.
Criminal justice personnel--Bahamas. 4. Crime--Bahamas. I. Title.

HV8170.5.A2 T56 2013
363.2097294-dc22

Editing and pre-press by Media Enterprises Ltd
31 Shirley Park Avenue
Tel: 242-325-8210
info@bahamasmedia.com   www.bahamasmedia.com

Contents

Dedication & Acknowledgements

This book is dedicated to all of my children and their families, whose contributions to my happiness and peace of mind are bountiful. The major part they played in my life in The Bahamas could never be fully recorded or adequately compensated.

It is with my profound gratitude that I recognise, acknowledge and applaud all the people in The Bahamas and this region who helped to make this book, the content of which is designed to educate and entertain.

I would like to specifically recognise those individuals and groups who were directly instrumental in my training and development during my years as a police officer, in particular the 25 years that I spent in the Criminal Investigation Department of the Royal Bahamas Police Force.

I cannot name all of them, but they know who they are. I am honoured to have served with you during the noble mission to make The Bahamas a safe and secure place for everyone.

Sir Albert Miller, Salathiel Thompson, Anthony Fields, Stanley Moir, Percy Campbell, Louis Hemmings, Gerrard Forrester (FBI), Fred Dick (DEA), and Gerald Bartlett.

Also the stress relievers - the Trini Posse and the Police Tennis and Domino Groups, including Dr. John Lunn, Dr. Cecil Bethel, Kemuel Hepburn and Neville Smith.

I wish to thank Eileen Dupuch Carron, publisher of the Tribune, for her support over the years and for producing a testimonial after reading this book. I also thank Larry Smith, longtime journalist and president of Media Enterprises, for his help and suggestions in editing my manuscript and getting this book published.

Foreword

THE Royal Bahamas Police Force was his university. It was where he received his professional education. It was also where he learned about teamwork, love for neighbour and colleagues, handling life's ups and downs, self-discipline and setting high personal standards.

It was here that he learned about jealousy, deceit, malice, hatred and all of those evils by which men can destroy themselves.

In these words retired assistant police commissioner Paul Thompson has given a synopsis of what 30 years as a proud member of the Royal Bahamas Police Force has meant to him.

"I came to the Bahamas a boy, and it was the Royal Bahamas Police Force that made me a man," he writes. "This book is neither an autobiography nor a history. It is my recollection of 30 years well spent."

It is a story well told of an interesting period of this small nation's progress to independence and beyond. And who better to tell it than this 86-year-old police officer, who has never ceased to show his gratitude to his adopted country for all the opportunities it has given him.

Even at this mature age, Paul Thompson is still close to the force, giving advice to the commissioner, to junior officers, to politicians, doing research for newspaper articles and writing letters on subjects that he thinks might improve the Bahamas' crime fighting abilities.

In one chapter he illustrates the importance of "keen observation and intelligent interrogation, followed by thorough investigation." Such police work resulted in the resolution of crimes that plagued the Montagu area years ago.

Then there was the Mackey Street shootout that involved one of the leading lights in the numbers racket, and a murder charge against Talbort Thompson, owner of the Corona Hotel, headquarters of his racket. The raid at Thompson's Mackey Street home, ended in a man being shot, and Thompson — after an "eloquent mercy plea from Gerald Cash" — receiving a light prison sentence.

One crime story follows another in this eclectic memoir. Thompson recounts the details of the Maxie murder — the English spinster secretary for HG Christie real estate — and the murder of Edward Grenidge, a Barbadian of English ancestry, who worked in the hotel industry.

Both were considered high profile cases, and Scotland Yard was brought in to solve them — much to the chagrin of Nassau's Criminal Investigation Department. The Maxie case was never solved, but CID had wrapped up the Grenidge case even before Scotland Yard arrived.

This book is a fascinating story of a highly respected police officer, born of a single mother —in those days, he says, they would have called him a "bastard" — in a remote village in Trinidad.

"I was loved by my parents and grandparents," Thompson recalled. "My father died when I was seven years old." He was "raised and nurtured" by his adoptive grandparents, Adoo Doon and her husband, Granville Pilgrim.

It was only by a fluke that he eventually became a Bahamian police officer. He was rejected several times, the first because he was an inch shorter than the required height. However, his prowess at sports eventually turned his fortunes.

The late Augustus "Gussie" Roberts was the recruiting officer, and under him, Thompson arrived in the Bahamas on Easter Sunday in 1951 to begin a new life and career.

Thompson has produced an interesting account of life in the Bahamas from the early fifties through independence and the drug wars to the present. It is a page turner that will not disappoint.

Eileen Carron,
Publisher, The Tribune

June 2013
Nassau, Bahamas

Introduction

Competitive sports and law enforcement were the most important influences on my life and career.

Ralph Legall was an outstanding West Indian sportsman who played cricket, soccer, table tennis and tennis for the Trinidad and Tobago national teams in the 1950s. He died in 2003, but I trained with him at the Woodbrook Youth Centre in Port of Spain.

Roy Armbrister was my sports mentor in The Bahamas. He excelled in cricket, soccer, boxing, swimming and track and field and was considered the greatest Bahamian sportsman of all time.

Randolph Burroughs and I were both apprentices at Trinidad Government Railways in the late 1940s, when we played cricket and soccer together on the Railways teams. Burroughs was Trinidad's Commissioner of Police from 1978 to 1987. During the early 70s, he was the leader of the flying squad, an elite police force that made a name for itself by stopping notorious criminals of the day in their tracks.

My early training in policing was supervised by Carlton Price Wentworth, who was seconded from Trinidad to the Bahamas Police Training School. Other outstanding officers who helped train me included Stanley Moir, Albert Miller, Salathial Thompson and Wenzel Granger - all highly respected senior officers.

My colleagues at the Criminal Investigation Department included Anthony Fields, Louis Hemmings, Fletcher Johnson, Courtney Strachan, Ormond Briggs, Milan Gittens, Lincoln Hercules, Egbert Eastmond, Douglas Hanna, Basil Dean, Arthur Yearwood, Bernard Bonamy, Kemuel Hepburn, Byron Simmons, Garbo Saunders, Lloyd Ifill, Carlyle Baptiste, Edney Johnson, Leroy Braithwaite, Darnley Jones and Fred Phillips.

J. Edgar Hoover was director of the US Federal Bureau of Investigation from 1935 (when the agency was founded) until his death on 1972 at the age of 77. Hoover is credited with building the FBI into a large and effective crime-fighting agency. He was a hero of mine, and although I never actually met Hoover, I did encounter several other FBI directors in the course of my career.

I worked closely with senior FBI agent Robert Peloquin on several high-profile cases in The Bahamas. Peloquin was an attorney who specialised in the investigation of organised crime and he became a legendary figure in the field of private intelligence. His firm, Intertel, was responsible for security at Resorts International and he also worked for billionaire Howard Hughes. He was instrumental in my appointment as head of security at the Paradise Island Resort & Casino in 1981. Peloquin died in 2011 at the age of 82.

My political views were strongly influenced by Dr Eric Williams, the eminent historian who became chief minister of Trinidad and Tobago in 1956 and remained in power until his death in 1981. His masterwork - *Capitalism and Slavery* - was published in 1944. In my view he was the region's most honest politician and was never tainted with corruption. He would never make promises that he knew could not be fulfilled.

Among Bahamian leaders, I had the greatest respect for Kendal Isaacs as a man of unflinching character, integrity and principle. He was not a good politician, but he was certainly a great judge and prosecutor. I also learned a lot from the writings of Etienne Dupuch, who was publisher of the Tribune from 1919 to 1972. He was a very courageous man, and his brother, Eugene, was a superlative defence attorney. Even when off-duty I would attend court to hear him address a jury.

A. F. Adderley was president of the Bahamas Cricket Association for many years and I was honoured to be able to speak to him from time to time. His son, Paul, was one of the best lawyers in the Bahamas and represented me gratis at an inquest into the death of a man I had arrested for multiple rapes. Orville Turnquest was also a big cricket fan and a good friend.

J Barrie Farrington was my boss at the Paradise Island Resort & Casino. He supported me fully in my efforts to upgrade security at the resort and we became close friends. I have also enjoyed a long friendship with George Myers, a Jamaican expatriate who achieved enormous business success in the Bahamas.

During my early career I had the opportunity to interact with outstanding magistrates like Wilton Hercules, John Bailey, Kenneth MacAllister, Max Thompson and Emmanuel Osadbay. It was always enlightening to visit their courts and read their judgements in important cases.

But the Royal Bahamas Police Force was my university. It is where I received my professional education. It is also where I learned about teamwork, love for neighbour and colleagues, handling life's ups and downs, self-discipline and setting high personal standards. It was where I learned about jealousy, deceit, malice, hatred and all of those evils by which men can destroy themselves.

I came to The Bahamas a boy, and it was the Royal Bahamas Police Force that made me a man. This book is neither an autobiography nor a history. It is my recollection of 30 years well spent.

Paul Thompson in uniform

CHAPTER 1

Cunupia Village

I was born 85 years ago in Cunupia village on Southern Main Road in Trinidad, not far from the farming town of Chaguanas. At the time the village had a population of less than 2,000 people, mostly of East Indian descent. Among the few prominent, but poor, black families were the Graingers, the Coombs, and my family - the Olivers, the Stephens and the Antoines.

We were farmers. My adoptive grandfather, Granville Pilgrim, was a former police officer from British Guiana (now Guyana) who had inherited land in Trinidad from his forefathers. We grew cocoa, coffee, sugarcane, fruit and ground provisions on land not far from our home.

My adoptive grandmother, Virginia Pilgrim (nee Samuels), was called Adoo Doon by the entire village. She was from the Amerindian tribe that had inhabited Trinidad before Columbus came. Virginia and Granville had been baptised and married in the local Roman Catholic Church. And they were able to provide a reasonably good living through farming.

Adoo Doon sold produce from our farm under the eave of a grocery shop on the village's main road. She also baked bread and cakes, washed clothes for the more prosperous people in the village, and maintained a rose garden, which provided extra money for our family. The cocoa, coffee and sugarcane revenue was not what was expected. The wholesalers in Port of Spain were most unfair to small farmers, and the sugar factories always underpriced our products.

I was born on the 19th of July, 1927 to a single mother named Lillian Oliver. My father was an architect and building contractor named Henry Seon Thompson. My mother helped Adoo Doon with the daily chores. In those days the child born to an unwed mother was called a "bastard", but I was loved by my parents and grandparents. I was the only child of both my parents. My father died when I was seven years old and I was raised and nurtured by Adoo Doon and Granville.

My mother eventually married Francis Bynoe, an engineer in the sugar cane factories, and moved to a place called Waterloo Village, which was closer to her husband's work. I was left in Cunupia where I was well cared for by my adoptive grandparents.

Cunupia Village, Chaguanas, Trinidad.

Other relatives included Aunts Rhoda of Laventille and Ethel of Port of Spain; and Uncle Ernest Oliver, who was a policeman. Relatives in Cunupia Village were Nelson Oliver, (my mother's father), and Uncle Bobby Oliver (Nelson's brother). They had a sister, who married a Chinese man and produced a large family of half-Chinese cousins, the Appings, who were entrepreneurs in transportation and refreshment stands.

Uncle Ernest had two beautiful daughters with a mulatto woman. He was dismissed from the police service and started a business making chocolate products. He purchased cocoa from grandpa and sold his products on the streets of Port of Spain. Uncle Ernest was a very jealous man and the woman he had the two daughters with was promiscuous. He subsequently committed suicide by jumping in front of a train.

Aunt Ethel lived in the city. She had three children - Barbara and the twins Aldwyn and Evelyn Oliver. The twins migrated to New York in their teens. Uncle Bobby had six children. They all lived in Cunupia Village and some of them are still there on Chin Chin Road. His youngest son, Sylvester, became the most famous in the Oliver family when he played international cricket for Trinidad & Tobago and was called to trials for the West Indies cricket team. He eventually migrated to England where he played professional cricket for decades.

Sylvester was my closest friend in the Oliver family. I spent time with him in England, and he and his wife visited me in Nassau. He died suddenly on a visit to Trinidad in 1999. We were together watching cricket just before he had a heart attack at his sister's home. My grandparents, my mother, aunts and uncles all died while I was living in The Bahamas.

I attended Cunupia Government School, where I excelled in sports - soccer, cricket, track and table tennis. I would have been accepted in a high school or college, but my grandparents could not afford the expense. There were very few scholarships available at that time, so I left school at age 14.

I went to work for my family, raising hogs and chickens and delivering bread

11

and cakes. I also did chores at a bakery in the village. My mother, who by this time had divorced her husband on the grounds of cruelty, was working as a housekeeper for the manager of United British Oilfields Trinidad (UBOT) in Point Fortin. My grandmother persuaded my mother to get me a job as an office boy and messenger in the Material Accounts Office at UBOT. I was there for a year and was promoted to filing clerk after learning to type and file documents.

I eventually lost this job due to an altercation with the office manager. I was polite, but stood my ground in the belief that I was right. I left Point Fortin a disappointed teenager and eventually ended up with Aunt Ethel and her kids in Nelson Street, Port of Spain, a slum area rife with youth gangs, prostitution and gambling. I was forced to live that environment, but never accepted it, making my own choices through work, adult education and sports.

At the age of 15 I got a job at a gas station on Wrightson Road in Port of Spain, where the United States military serviced their vehicles. Between adult classes and sports I had no time to be on the blocks or engage with the young toughs in the area. It was from work to the classroom or sports field.

Adoo Doon was not happy about my exposure to the evil things in the neighbourhood. So she encouraged my mother to leave her job in Point Fortin and relocate to Port of Spain. She and I moved to a rented house in Belmont, a suburb of the capital. When I was 16 she urged me to take an apprenticeship at the Trinidad Government Railways as a machinist on a five-year contract.

Although I learned and performed well (as reported by the engineers) as an apprentice, I was unhappy with the wages. But the job gave me the opportunity to play on various sport teams, and travel to British Guiana in 1948 to play cricket, soccer, table tennis and volleyball. That was my first trip outside of Trinidad. I was also invited to trials to play table tennis for Trinidad.

Sports and my family's policing background must have prompted my decision to leave Trinidad for the Royal Bahamas Police Force. One Sunday morning in Cunupia, we had just finished playing soccer against a visiting team from another village when I was seated under a tree near to the street. The Trinidad Guardian van stopped to deliver papers and I bought one and saw a story indicating that The Bahamas had sent a police officer named Gussie Roberts to recruit personnel for their force. I immediately expressed my interest and committed myself to pursuing my recruitment.

When I told my grandparents of my decision, they knew nothing of The Bahamas and tried to get me to join the Police Service in Trinidad. But eventually they consented and offered their prayers, advising me to work hard and be honest. So I got permission from my boss at the Railways to pursue my dream and proceeded to the Police Training School in St. James. But it was no easy thing.

At the college I met about a thousand other young men on the line, but the numbers were immensely reduced when a senior officer speaking from a loudspeaker, announced that anyone with

Augustus Roberts

major or minor convictions, who was married or had children, or who had previously served in the Trinidad Police, would not be accepted. The remaining applicants were then measured and weighed.

My weight was acceptable, but I was one inch less than the approved height of 5' 9", so I failed to advance. I saw a sergeant, who knew me from sports, and he advised me to go to the gym and do some stretching exercises. I did and got some advice from the gym operator on how to stand to make up that inch. On the following day I went back to the Police College and submitted myself for the height check. I made the inch and was sent to the police doctor for my physical.

I have a large scar on my left leg from a childhood train accident that nearly took my life, so the doctor immediately disqualified me. When I told him of my ability in sports he asked for written proof and I was able to obtain letters from the soccer, cricket, table tennis, track & field and volleyball associations of Trinidad & Tobago. Also, it turned out that the police physician had interned under the doctor who had originally treated my leg.

So I passed the physical, and the educational test was simple. We were told to return on the following day for the results, but I did not hear my name called. The examiner, Inspector Hunt, happened to be my godfather, but he had not seen me since childhood. He recognised the names of my parents on the application and told me that I had got a100% pass, but failed the maths test as I did not show how I arrived at the answers, although they were all correct. I told him my employment in the railways and classes at the Royal Victoria Institute kept me sharp and math had been used daily in my job. He agreed to pass me.

The final stage of the process was an interview with Gussie Roberts. He told me that The Bahamas needed 12 men and there were 18 candidates, so he had to leave six and I was not one of those selected. I asked him to give the six of us first consideration in the future, which he undertook to do. Disappointed again, I returned to my job on the railways.

But the following week I was told that a police officer wanted to see me. I thought I was being collared for cycling through a traffic policeman's stop signal earlier that week, but the officer asked me if I was still interested in The Bahamas job. Of course, I accepted and was instructed to get a passport. My long-awaited departure for Nassau was scheduled for Easter Saturday morning 1951, on Pan American World Airways. It would be my first flight ever.

I was able to collect my provident fund payments and wages, and my colleagues presented gifts before I reported to the Trinidad Police Barracks at 10pm on Good Friday night to sleep in. I had spent most of my money on clothing and gave my mother some cash, so that I only had about $10 for travel. My mother said I should ask my godmother for financial assistance, but she lived in San Fernando some 40 miles away and the $10 would not take me there. So I hitched a ride to Cunupia to ask a friend to drive me to San Fernando, but he was gambling and wouldn't leave the game. Luckily, I joined the game and in a short time my $10 stake had grown to $250.

On the following morning - Easter Saturday 1951- I left for The Bahamas. We overnighted in Jamaica as guests of the police there, and arrived in Nassau on Easter Sunday at the Oakes Field airport. My new life and career had begun.

The police barracks on East Street was formerly the prison. A 17-man police force was established in 1840, operating from a single station house on Parliament Street. A paramilitary constabulary was set up in 1891, to replace the departing West India Regiment. In 1909, the police merged with the constabulary force for a total strength of 129 officers.

CHAPTER 2

Arrival in The Bahamas

My new home was the old police barracks on East Street - a British Army-style building with dormitories on two levels equipped with bunk beds. Recruits were housed together in specific rooms. There were 18 of us, including five Bahamians - Lawrence Major (who later became an assistant commissioner), Ivan Rahming, Ulysses Pratt, Anton Coleby and Joba Peterson. It did not take long for us to become fast friends and a disciplined team.

The barracks building also housed the Police Training School in the northern end of the basement, the Police Club in the middle of the basement, and a storeroom on the southern end. Police headquarters, with the commissioner's office, and the pay office, were in a nearby building. The main guard operated from the ground floor. To the south and southwest of the barracks was the prison; to the north was the commissioner's residence and other buildings housing foreign senior officers. At the rear was the drill parade.

The Police Club was an oasis where off-duty officers congregated for relaxation, beverages, and snacks (usually corned beef and tuna sandwiches). We trained in the mornings under Cyril Smith, a prominent Bahamian body builder, with either a three-mile run to Fort Montagu or aerobic exercises on the drill parade. This regimen started at 5.30 am. Breakfast was at 7.30 am, at a small restaurant across the street, and at 8 there were drills with the old heavy 303 rifles. These were led by a British Army drill expert named Atkinson. Both Smith and Atkinson were very good instructors. Apart from the drills we were taught how to clean rifles and revolvers.

At 9 am we assembled in the classroom for training by a remarkable man named Carlton Price Wentworth, an inspector who had been seconded to the Bahamian police from Trinidad. He was the best teacher I ever encountered. I had a grandfather and two uncles in the Guyanese and Trinidad police, but it was through Wentworth that I developed my long-lasting love for police work.

In the ensuing months, I met many people who I came to admire and respect. Major Eddie Sears, a man whose courage and integrity made him unpopular with the people of power and denied him promotion to the rank of commissioner for many years. His report in the Harry Oakes murder case was unacceptable to the political hierarchy

Reginald Dumont   Keith Mason   Sir Albert Miller   Courtney Strachan

of the time. There was also Spencer Harty, an English deputy commissioner. Wenzel Grainger and Gussie Roberts were in charge of B and A Divisions respectively, and were both excellent Bahamian officers who had served in the British Army and were well respected. Sergeant Stanley Blair was in charge of the pay office and Gerald Bartlett was a clerk in the pay office.

Card games and checkers were played regularly in the Police Club, and the recruits from Trinidad joined in outdoor sports like cricket, soccer, track and field, and eventually table tennis. And with the help of Wentworth, Blair, Bartlett and others, the Police Sports Club was formed. Sir George Roberts, a prominent politician at the time, donated all of the cricket gear. It was during this period that I met for the first time that great Bahamian sportsman Roy Armbrister, who was then a police sergeant. Armbrister was successful in almost every sport he played, although he was best known for his cricketing skills. He also became heavyweight boxing champion, and was an exceptional soccer player, sprinter and long-distance swimmer. This remarkable man was to become my mentor in sports and discipline when he was selected to captain the police cricket team, which included our recruit squad and players such as Segfried Wilson, Reginald Dumont, Harold Lecky and Errington Watkins.

The police cricket team was unbeaten in its first season, and we entered the local soccer league and won there too. We went on to excel in table tennis and were champions for a few years of competition at the Priory. Police involvement in local sports was considered good for public relations, and when Acting Commissioner Eddie Sears retired in 1955, the sports club was a major part of his legacy.

Sears was replaced by Colchester Wemyss, who took police sporting activities to an even higher level. He found a good supporter in Inspector Les Cates. The police sporting field was born and so were the tennis courts, the senior officers' mess and the banquets held in the barracks for Christmas and New Year's.

Our squad of recruits completed training in October 1951. At the Passing Out Parade I met the governor - Brigadier-General Sir Robert Neville - and I was impressed. After graduation I spent seven months in the B Division of the Uniform Branch under Wenzel Grainger and Daniel "Blood" Mason, a Jamaican officer. We spent many dreary hours on sentry duty at the barracks and at Government House. A sentry would stand for hours on his post with a heavy rifle. To relieve stress he would occasionally patrol a prescribed area. Sentries were marched to Government House and would patrol from the eastern to the western gate. When I was on sentry duty, the governor at the time - Sir

Stanley Moir   Basil Dean   Milan Gittens   Douglas Hanna

Robert Neville, a former brigadier-general in the British Army - would often come out to chat with the sentries in the early hours of the morning.

But I was soon selected by Grainger to be a part of a squad to go after persons involved in the Numbers racket. Reggie Dumont was also a part of the team. The Numbers is a game of chance that dates back to 16th century Europe and has been popular in the Bahamas since the 1800s at least. It is associated with poor communities around the world because punters can bet small sums of money and get credit from their bookies. The first anti-gambling law in the Bahamas was enacted in 1901, and was gradually strengthened to create an absolute ban on lotteries and gaming houses - except for specific exemptions awarded to charity raffles and a handful of resort casinos, where only tourists could gamble. In June 1952, Reggie Dumont and I were posted to the Criminal Investigation Department, as detectives on probation. And it was here that I began to realise my full potential in policing. At CID I met outstanding officers like Salathiel Thompson (who became the first post-Independence police commissioner) and Albert Miller, who became one of the kingpins of Freeport after retiring from the force in the 1970s. It was Thompson who monitored my probation as a detective while Miller tutored me. There were also officers like Carl Glinton, George Moncur, Oswald Ashby, Mervyn Hutchinson, Courtney Strachan and Richard Ellis, to name a few.

Salathiel Thompson was very hard on me. So much so that I feared I would have to return to the Uniform Branch at the end of my probation. But when I saw the report he wrote on my performance I actually broke down and wept. It was a glowing testament in which he and Albert Miller both expressed their pride in my accomplishments and commended my dedication and discipline.

Alardyce Strachan   Sheila Armbrister   Ormond Briggs   Lawrence Major

My detective training continued under Frank Russell, who came to us from Scotland Yard, as well as under the master detective Stanley Moir, who took me under his wing. Originally from Sunderland, England, Moir arrived in the Bahamas in 1956 as an assistant superintendant on a transfer from the Bermuda police. He rose to become assistant commissioner before retiring in 1986, and died in 2012. It was Moir who checked all of my investigation reports, adding his comments and a list of to do's before the cases could be closed. He often cited me for commendations and usually selected me for trips to the Family Islands to conduct investigations. He appreciated the fact that my expense accounting was never too high, and I most often got the desired results.

At that time in CID we had no specific fraud squad, drug squad or murder squad. Detectives had to investigate all types of crimes. There was no Special Branch either at that time, and we were also expected to provide information on labour matters as well as protection for VIPs. Moir's team included detectives Ormond Briggs, Milan Gittens, Lincoln Hercules, Egbert Eastmond, McDonald Chase, Fletcher Johnson, Louis Hemmings, Willis Bullard, Basil Dean, Douglas Hanna, Arthur Yearwood, Sheila Armbrister, Alardyce Strachan, Avery Ferguson and many others who were once colleagues of mine.

The sergeant in charge was the very efficient and effective Anthony "Dog" Fields, who was also from Trinidad. He was a good teacher and led the younger detectives by example. He made a remarkable contribution to crime fighting and detective training in the Bahamas, although he never got the promotions he deserved. Fields was the first commandant of the Police College, which was a donation from the British government.

I spent most of my career in criminal investigation. At first there was a stint of 17 consecutive years, followed by another eight years as an assistant commissioner. At least two former commissioners wanted to know how I was able to get detectives to work the extra duties without complaint. The answer was simple - they were all dedicated to their job and were treated like human beings. They were also part of the team left by great officers like Frank Russell and Stanley Moir.

CHAPTER 3

A Chance to Advance

In the early years of my career there were no computers. We had a Crime Book, in which all complaints were recorded, including progress reports. Most information was written in blue ink, with arrests written in red. Senior personnel in the Criminal Investigation Department monitored the book daily, and very often gave written directions to investigating officers on how to progress with their investigations.

There was a book for each month of the year. At the end of the month the superintendent would prepare statistics on the number of crimes reported and the results of the investigations. From this it was clear which detectives were solving the most cases and making arrests. And I am unashamed to say that I was always among the leaders.

The main vehicle used by detectives in the 1950s was the bicycle. Besides providing basic transportation, it helped to maintain our health and fitness. The single motor vehicle was consigned to the Fingerprint and Photography Unit headed by B.J. Nottage, who was also responsible for the Criminal Records Office. On his team were Maurice Smith and a fellow Trinidadian named MacDonald "Porog" Chase. Nottage was a very efficient officer and a good teacher. He was the father of Kendal Nottage and Dr. Bernard Nottage, and was considered the best-dressed policeman on the Force.

Senior personnel in CID were impressed with my record of solving cases as a junior detective. In those days most cases were burglaries since violent crime was uncommon. Murder was so rare that the superintendent handled all those investigations personally.

Bernard J. Nottage

Salathiel Thompson and Albert Miller were detective sergeants in CID at the time. Thompson was also an exceptional prosecutor in the Magistrate's Court. Very often when I was not engaged, I would visit the court to listen to him debate with leading defense attorneys like Eugene Dupuch, Loran Pyfrom, Gerald Cash and others. It was a learning experience for me.

One rainy morning I arrived for work early and was informed by B.J. Nottage of a burglary at Little Orchard on Village Road, an upscale cottage resort. I cycled to the scene of the crime and interviewed the victim - who happened to be the Canadian Minister of Finance. He was a good friend of Sir Stafford Sands, a powerful Nassau politician and attorney at the time.

The Canadian was here with his wife and young child, and he was naturally concerned for his family's safety. The cottage had been entered through a bathroom window, and the burglar had removed a wallet from the dresser and an envelope from a table in the living room. The wallet and the envelope contained a total of $6,000 in cash, and we knew the exact denominations in both Canadian and American currency. It was his first night in Nassau and the Canadian had kept a written record of his cash. When the area around the cottage was searched we found the wallet on the other side of a wall, but no fingerprints were obtained.

Photocopying machines did not exist in those days, so back at the office I used carbon paper to copy the denominations of the stolen money and delivered a copy to every bank in Nassau. Most were on Bay Street, but the Penny Savings Bank and Bodie Bank were over-the-hill. I had to report the results of the crime scene investigation directly to the superintendent, who promptly informed the commissioner, Major Eddie Sears. I recall there being some miscommunication between Stafford Sands' office and police headquarters relative to providing a guard at the cottage occupied by the minister and his family.

The following morning I received a telephone call from a Mr. Waddams of Barclays Bank. He told me there was a white woman making a deposit with bills similar to the denominations listed on my memo. I went to the bank and interviewed the woman, who was employed by a Canadian developer building homes in the Chippingham area. She told me a man had visited her office the day before and bought two lots, using the cash she was depositing as a downpayment. The buyer, a man named Granville Cooper, carried this money in an envelope, which I was able to locate in the trash at the woman's office. I then went to see the land that Cooper had purchased, being advised by Albert Miller not to arrest the suspect without help as he was known to be violent and had only recently been released from prison. In fact, he had only recently visited CID to report a stolen bicycle.

I rode to the lot on my police bicycle and saw a man with a cutlass, whom I took to be Cooper. I told him we were holding someone who had been found with Cooper's stolen bicycle but who claimed he had bought it. At this Cooper became angry, hid the cutlass in the bush, and accompanied me to CID, which was temporarily housed at police headquarters. I took him directly to Albert Miller, who had collected the stolen money from Barclay's Bank. Miller presented the money to Cooper and asked him where he got the cash for a downpayment on the land in Chippingham. At the same time I placed the envelope on Miller's desk in full view of Cooper, who gave me a very angry look and suddenly fell to the floor in a faint.

Cooper was charged with the burglary and theft. When the news reached Stafford Sands I was asked to report to his law office, where he and the Canadian minister commended me for good police work. Sands said there was no monetary reward, but something would happen in due course. And in about two months I was promoted from junior detective to the rank of lance corporal. One day I was the junior man on the shift and the next I was in charge of the shift.

Meanwhile, Granville Cooper was returned to Her Majesty's Prison to serve a long term while I was commended by the trial judge. This marked the real beginning of my career as a detective. The promotion opened doors for me, and soon I was being sent to the out islands to investigate serious crimes. I travelled often to Jamaica to get lab work done, and in 1958 I was seconded to the West Riding Detective Training School in Yorkshire, England, where I emerged fifth in a class of about 30 officers from the UK, Asia and Africa. I was on the move!

Early police training was little more drill and instruction on how to use a truncheon. But in 1926 a detective training programme was established by the local chief constable, at West Riding in Yorkshire, and this provided a model for future police academies in Britain, teaching the latest technologies.

The basic training I received in Nassau as a police recruit helped me to understand the on-the-job training I later received at CID. That training, and working with quality police officers, helped me to appreciate the further training I received in England. The months I spent at the school in Yorkshire were a very worthwhile learning experience, giving me the opportunity to compete and exchange ideas with officers from many other countries.

The programme included extensive training in crime scene investigation and I was exposed to the latest techniques and forensic procedures. It became clear to me just how much evidence could be lost if crime scenes were not approached expertly, with patience and alertness. I was taught to be mindful that criminals always make mistakes, but it is only through training and sharp observation that investigators can find those mistakes.

Upon my return to the Bahamas I immediately began sharing this newly acquired knowledge with my colleagues. And in the ensuing months, crime scene examination improved dramatically, especially in cases involving rapes. Our use of the laboratories at the Princess Margaret hospital became more frequent, and it was noted by the lab technician at the time (Clement Maynard, who later became a senior government minister) and the pathologists (Doctors Read and Duck) that they were being asked to provide much more detailed information in their post mortem reports.

The first opportunity to use my newly acquired forensic skills involved a homicide on Eleuthera. Two men were involved in a fight inside a house. One died and the other left the scene surreptitiously. Investigation in the neighbourhood disclosed that the deceased was visited frequently by a man, whose name was given. At the scene I secured bloodstained clothing and, most importantly, skin from under the fingernails of the deceased. I used the methods I had learned in Britain to secure the evidence. The skin under the nails indicated that the suspect would have been scratched during the fight.

We eventually found the suspect, who had visible scratches on his neck. But he denied visiting the deceased on the day of the murder and said the scratches were from walking in thick bush. There were other marks on his body, which indicated suspected violence, and we found that he too had skin under his nails. This evidence was also secured, and everything was sent to the police laboratory in Jamaica. Their report supported our suspicion that the two men had been in a fight, and when this conclusion was put to the suspect in the presence of his attorney he confessed and was subsequently charged and convicted of manslaughter.

Overseas training for police officers is rewarding for both the individuals involved and for the Force as a whole. Many of our better officers were UK-trained, including Albert Miller, Courtney Strachan, Anthony Fields and others who advanced to senior positions. McDonald Chase, whom the FBI considered to be the best fingerprint expert in the Caribbean, was trained at the same West Riding school that I attended, and the detective training programme of the Royal Bahamas Police Force was based on this programme.

The value of such training was underscored in a 1995 review, which included the following comment: "The increasing interconnectedness of the world (means that) law enforcement organizations like the Royal Bahamas Police Force must take proactive approaches to crime. The training and retraining of staff and collaborative efforts between law enforcement agencies locally and internationally are needed to effectively combat the harsh realities globalization will bring to The Bahamas and the region."

CHAPTER 4

A Serial Rapist in East Nassau

In the 1950s and early 1960s, Nassau was a very pleasant place to live, work or visit. Crime was minimal, violent crime was rare, and the general population was friendly and disciplined.

There were several night clubs, and the best of them were located over-the-hill. Both locals and visitors from downtown hotels very often walked to these clubs. Imagine being able to walk through Grants Town and Bain Town to the Cat & Fiddle Club on Nassau Street without fear of being molested - and to be able to enjoy the entertainment, without being subjected to fights or disorderly conduct. In those days police patrols were constant and loiterers were not permitted outside any of the clubs, so tourists were unlikely to be solicited by vendors or drug pushers. In any event, back then the community was relatively drug free.

Illicit activities included so-called "30-day joints" (places where liquor was sold without a licence), gambling joints (usually in bar rooms), and the Numbers racket,. There were occasional shop-breakings and burglaries, as well as fraudulent land sales, forged cheques and employee thefts. It was enough to keep the Criminal Investigation Department busy, but not overloaded. At the time, the department included a superintendent, an inspector, two sergeants and about 10 detectives. There was the occasional flying squad, under the command of Edney Johnson, that was used for foot patrols in areas where there were shop-breakings and burglaries. The Vagrancy Act was a very important weapon, and was frequently used by the flying squad to arrest loiterers in areas where crime was prevalent.

For example, one year it became obvious to us from the number of reports received, that the serenity of East Bay Street and the Eastern Road was threatened. This area was populated by the local white elite and wealthy English residents. Women were being raped in the bush along the Eastern Road from as far west as the silk worm farm (now the Harbour Bay Shopping Centre) to as far east as Deal's Heights.

These rapes occurred during the early morning hours when young housemaids were walking to work. There was no jitney transportation in that area at the time. The assailant would hide in the bush, grab a passerby and threaten her with a long knife, while raping her. The descriptions given by the victims were all very similar: a man in his late teens or early twenties, of slim build and dark brown complexion, who was very strong and physically fit.

The flying squad was deployed to the area to conduct surveillance at numerous locations. Detectives displayed photos of known rapists to the victims in an effort to get an identification, which proved fruitless. Then the attacks began occurring in the mid-afternoon and early evenings, but the *modus operandi* remained the same and the description of the attacker was always the same. Detective Louis Hemmings and I were deployed to patrol the general area in an old army jeep from dusk to dawn.

The victims of the afternoon and evening attacks were also mostly housemaids, but they now included students walking home from school. In one incident, the victim was the teenage granddaughter of an English aristocrat living on the Eastern Road (she was on vacation here at the time). This placed a great deal of pressure on CID to solve the case. I had always been taught, that criminals will always make mistakes and it was up to the investigating officers to detect those errors, which would inevitably lead to the arrest of the criminal. I did not believe that luck had anything to do with it, but my colleagues considered me to be lucky.

In this instance, we conducted the most thorough investigation possible, ensuring that all of the basic routines were followed. We re-visited every rape scene to search for anything that may have been discarded, such as tissue paper or clothing. But despite our efforts we were unable to crack the case.

One sunny morning Hemmings and I re-visited the scene of a recent rape at Montagu, but again came up with nothing. As we drove back to CID Hemmings noticed a man climbing over the silk worm farm wall onto East Bay Street, who jumped back over the wall as soon as he saw our police jeep. I stopped the jeep and ran over to the wall. The man was running towards Shirley Street so I jumped the wall and gave chase. My sports training in track, soccer and cricket proved helpful, and I was able to catch up just as he was about to jump the Shirley Street wall. I grabbed him, but his momentum pulled me over the wall on top of him.

At that point I was in an intense struggle with a strong man wielding a knife - but I knew we had collared the rapist. It was up to me to hold on to him. I held the hand with the knife to keep it away from me while hollering loudly for help. The suspect got on top of me and I was about to lose my grip on his knife hand when he suddenly relaxed and slumped over me. Hemmings had clipped him behind the head with a blackjack that he carried.

With the suspect safely unconscious, we handcuffed him and proceeded to the hospital when he regained consciousness. There was no doubt in my mind that he was the serial rapist. The descriptions of both the man and the knife given by victims fitted well.

We held an identification parade to which all of the victims participated except the granddaughter of the English aristocrat, who did not want her to be identified as a rape victim. All of the other women identified the suspect, whose name was Rolle, and one of the victims physically attacked him and had to be restrained.

Rolle was sentenced to life imprisonment and ordered to receive strokes with the cat-o'-nine tails. Hemmings and I were both commended by the commissioner and later by the court. I told my colleagues, who liked to call me lucky, that our return to the crime scene on that particular morning just happened to put us in the right place at the right time. After that it was keen observation, immediate pursuit, determination and physical fitness that enabled us to make the arrest. Rolle's dramatic capture made the headlines, and the names Hemmings and Thompson received worthy mention.

CHAPTER 5

The Death of Raymond Burns

It was shortly after midnight when Detective Sergeant Ingram Ford visited my home on Lewis Street to ask for help with the investigation of two rapes in (month of) 1958. It was clear from descriptions of the assailant and the modus operandi involved that both rapes were committed by the same individual.

In those years the night shift at CID ran from 9pm to 9am and consisted of three detectives, including a corporal in charge. One detective kept the diary in the office, while the other two patrolled and responded to complaints. They worked an 84-hour week. The day shift worked a 60-hour week. There was a single unmarked police vehicle for the entire department, and no communications equipment other than the telephone.

When an arrest was made, the first order of business was to get the suspect to the police station. Very often helpful citizens would call the station and a police vehicle would be sent to assist. As a detective - and because of my general attitude, discipline and participation in sports -I was very popular with taxi drivers. They respected me for being discreet, which gave me the ability to get information from persons who wished to remain confidential. There were times when I was asked by senior officers to disclose the source of information, but I always respectfully declined.

So on that August night in 1958 I left with Sergeant Ford to interview the two women who had been raped. One told me the assailant had threatened her with a large screwdriver and the other said a metal file had been placed into her vagina. They had already been treated for minor injuries at the hospital. Both women had been at the Conch Shell Club on the night of the rapes, so I proceeded to Blue Hill Road South on a police motor scooter, armed with a 45-calibre revolver loaded with six rounds of ammunition.

Detectives did not normally carry weapons in those days, but I was the chief witness in a celebrated sedition case against Randol Fawkes, the popular labour leader who was facing trial after leading a general strike in January that had been sparked by the Taxi Cab Union. Officers who were involved in his arrest had received death threats, which were always taken seriously by the police. The governor had therefore approved the issue of firearms to detectives Carl Glinton, Courtney Strachan and myself, for our protection.

At the Conch Shell Club I spoke to the manager and several taxi drivers, describing the two female patrons and the truck that the rapist apparently drove. Two cab drivers told me they had seen a white Cavalier Construction truck parked on the street outside the club on two occasions earlier in the night.

I knew a man named Simeon Bowe, who worked at Cavalier. I went to interview him at his home on Christie Street and he told me that no one had use of the company truck after hours, but they had long suspected it was being removed at night from their compound at Shirley Park Avenue. He suggested waiting by the compound to see if the truck was returned before work began later that morning.

The truck eventually arrived at Shirley Park Avenue, but on seeing me the driver did not stop. He drove on to the roundabout at the dead-end and returned at speed. I followed on my motor scooter, travelling east on Shirley Street. The truck side-swiped three cars before turning south onto Kemp Road where it suddenly stopped, but I was able to avoid both the truck and a wall. The truck proceeded along Kemp Road and into the Five Pound Lot area where it ran off the road and collided with a tree.

From a safe distance I told the driver to get out of the truck. He appeared to be searching for something, so I displayed my firearm and told him he was under arrest for removing a vehicle without permission of the owner. After some persuasion he emerged from the truck. Residents in the area, who had heard the collision were emerging from their homes to see what was going on. A large crowd eventually appeared on the street, but I could not see anyone I could call on for help, so I decided that I would have to leave the scooter and walk my prisoner to the nearest police station, which at that time was on East Bay Street. But as I was about to leave, a passing taxi driver, who was a police cricket team fan, stopped and offered me a ride. Relieved, I placed the suspect in the front seat between the driver and myself.

As the taxi was about to drive off the suspect elbowed me in the face and grabbed for the gun in my waistband. I was able to hold on to his arm, keeping the barrel pointed away from me, as we wrestled our way onto the back seat of the cab where I was able to get on top of him. I saw an American sailor with a local white prostitute near the taxi and shouted for them to open the back door of the vehicle, which they did. I was then able to get my feet outside on the ground and pull the suspect towards me, still keeping the gun barrel pointed away from me. During this struggle a shot was fired and the gun was released. The suspect fell just outside the back door of the taxi and was declared dead by the time we arrived at the hospital emergency room.

What happened next was a test of my discipline as a police officer, my faith in God, my ability to recall details, and my faith in my colleagues - who were delegated to investigate the death.

I was standing outside the hospital when the Superintendent of CID, a white Englishman, arrived. In a frightening tone of voice he ordered me to hand over the gun and return to the office immediately. There was no further conversation.

At CID I was assigned to clerical duties while Sergeants Carl Glinton and George Moncur began investigating my encounter with the suspect. Bystanders at the time of the incident claimed I was standing several feet away from the suspect when I shot him after taking aim, but the distances given varied. The investigating officers were familiar with many of the people involved because they had been arrested before for playing the numbers. The prostitute gave an accurate version of what happened on that morning. She also gave the name of the sailor she was with and he was able to verify her story. He said I had called on him to open the car door and that a shot was fired during the struggle for the gun. The taxi driver confirmed that the suspect had hit me with his elbow and grabbed for my gun. Meanwhile, the rape victims were able to identify the suspect in the mortuary.

Upon completion of the investigation I was told of the overwhelming evidence against me of those witnesses who lived in the area, and was advised to retain a lawyer for the coroner's inquest that would soon be held. I had come to know Paul Adderley through cricket, and had also seen him at work in the courts, and I considered him one of the best legal minds in the country. I knew he would be able to put a dent in the testimony of the witnesses in the area who were fabricating stories about the incident.

The inquest was conducted by Magistrate Maxwell Thompson. There was a representative from the Attorney-General's Office and the police prosecutor. I was represented by Mr Adderley. I recall going to see him in his Frederick Street chambers to retain his services. He greeted me with: "You kill the man and now you come to see me?" He would not tell me what his services would cost.

At the inquest the people from the area gave their evidence, but under intense cross-examination it appeared that the jurors were unimpressed. It also appeared, that the Coroner believed they were perjuring themselves as he warned them of the consequences. The prostitute corroborated my report of the incident, and the sailor's affidavit was read, which also supported my story.

But the evidence that saved me came from the hospital pathologist, Dr. Duck, who testified that the trajectory of the bullet was downwards and that if it had been fired from any of the distances stated the trajectory would have been upwards. He also reported powder burns on the suspect's clothing and skin, which indicated that the shot was fired from very close range. This expert testimony clinched the case, and the coroner reprimanded the witnesses for their fabrications. The verdict of the jury was "death by misadventure."

Burns, alias Mong, had spent several years in jail for previous crimes and was known to be a violent person. But it was a valuable learning experience for me to sit in court and listen to the lies told by those witnesses. It was evident that they were upset by my consistent performance as a policeman and wanted to get rid of me even if it meant my serving a term in prison.

It was my first experience of the malice and hatred held by criminals for police officers, and thereafter I made every effort to protect myself from exposure to such threats.

CHAPTER 6

Crime in Wealthy Montagu Heights

In 1959 the affluent Village Road/Montagu Heights area had become the target of thieves operating during the day while residents were at work. One of the houses broken into was the home of the Comptroller of Customs, who was a collector of expensive watches. About half a dozen watches - with gold wristbands - had been stolen.

In response to this crime wave, the CID had mounted special daylight patrols in the area, both on foot and on bicycles. On these patrols we looked for people in areas where they did not live or work, and questioned them as to why they were in the particular area. Failure to give a reasonable explanation could result in a charge of vagrancy.

One particular day I was on patrol with Anthony Fields when we observed three boys of school age sitting under a tree in Montagu Heights. We stopped and pretended to ask them the whereabouts of someone living in the area. As we conversed we edged closer to the boys, so that by the time they tried to run we were able to grab three of them.

One of the boys was wearing a gold wristwatch and another had a pair of gold cuff-links in his pocket. The third boy carried 20 pounds in cash. We took them to the CID office for interrogation and invited the Comptroller of Customs to identify the watch found on the boy, which he did. In fact, his initials were engraved on the back of the watch.

Other items that had been stolen from homes in the area included jewellery, radios and cash. Interrogation prior to the identification of the wristwatch by the Customs chief was not encouraging. One boy said he had received the watch as a gift. The second said his mother had given him the 20 pounds, and the third said the cuff-links belonged to his father.

In checking their stories with the parents it became clear that they were not telling the truth. According to their parents, the boys had left for school that morning and that is where they should have been. But a check with the school revealed they had been absent on several recent occasions, and those dates corresponded to the reports of break-ins in Montagu Heights. We were satisfied we were on course to solve these crimes. In the second round of interrogation we were able to put all of this information to the boys, and they decided to tell us the true story.

They implicated a white boy living in Pyfrom's Addition, who was a student at the same school. They accompanied us to Montagu Heights and pointed out all the houses that had been broken into. We executed warrants on their homes and were able to recover some of the stolen items, but the comptroller's remaining watches were not found. So we visited the home of the Pyfrom's Addition boy with a search warrant and told his mother about the investigation. She denied that her son was involved in such crime, but the boy was found wearing a gold wristwatch of the type reported stolen by the comptroller. Neither mother nor son could account for their possession of the watch, so we arrested the boy.

Upon further interrogation we learned from the boys that three of the watches stolen from the comptroller's home had been sold to a white shopkeeper on East Shirley Street for five pounds. We searched his shop and home with a warrant, accompanied by our resident search expert - a Jamaican named Louis Hemmings. The shopkeeper claimed the boys were lying on him, and in the house we found nothing incriminating. But in the shop there was a stock of rice stored in a tin on a low shelf, and the suspect became very nervous when Hemmings removed this container. Emptying the contents on the counter we found three gold watches, which were valued at about 500 pounds each and were all positively identified later by the Customs chief.

The shopkeeper was charged and convicted of receiving stolen goods, while the boys were convicted in the juvenile court. The supreme court judge who tried the shopkeeper's case was very harsh with him for encouraging criminality amongst young people. He was sentenced to two year's imprisonment at hard labour. Each of the boys received strokes with the tamarind switch.

Keen observation and intelligent interrogation, followed by thorough investigation, resulted in the resolution of this spate of crimes. Hemmings was a master of the search who could find anything hidden anywhere. He was so often to prove an asset to CID.

CHAPTER 7

The Mackey Street Shootout

The Numbers racket has been widespread on New Providence for many decades. In my day, Bahamians bought numbers from street vendors, or in bars and petty shops over-the-hill. Some number sellers visited offices, shops and other businesses to provide customised services.

Buyers would choose a number (often based on their dreams) and the number seller would give him a piece of paper with his selection on it. The seller would record the name of the buyer in a notebook for reference when the draw was made. This differed from the present day operations, in which the numbers are drawn outside of The Bahamas, usually in the United States, and all of the administrative work is done by computers.

Back then, the Numbers houses held the draws locally - except for the Cuban lottery, which was drawn in Havana every Saturday and broadcast over Cuban radio stations received in The Bahamas. There were three main Numbers houses on New Providence operated by very wealthy individuals - Talbot Thompson, Percy Munnings and Eugene Toote.

Apart from their Numbers houses, Thompson and Munnings were known to be involved in heavy personal gambling, often winning or losing small fortunes in a single night. In later years, Father Allen, a well-known restaurant owner, established a fourth Numbers house. All of these men are now dead.

Thompson was a flamboyant character who drove around in a Cadillac convertible smoking expensive cigars. On his frequent visits downtown he would stop at all the police stations, where he would be met outside by various officers to whom he would give money. He had a reputation for corrupting the police.

Thompson owned several businesses and a lot of real estate on New Providence. His main business was the infamous Corona Club on Bay Street, just west of Deveaux Street. This building housed a nightclub, restaurant and bar, as well as a station to buy numbers and a place where the winning numbers were drawn. The bar was frequented by prostitutes and when warships were visiting the port of Nassau, servicemen would flock to the Corona in search of entertainment. In those years, the police rarely entered the premises.

Percy Munnings was more low-key. He too owned a lot of real estate as well as two liquor stores and a club on Wulff Road where the numbers were drawn and where the night gambling occurred. But he was a quiet and well-mannered man who did little to attract attention to himself. He made large donations to sporting activities, especially cricket, which he loved to play and watch.

For years Munnings would take a Bahamian cricket team to compete in Jamaica. Eventually, he discontinued these trips to give full support to the Wanderers Cricket Club on its tours to Canada, the United States, the West Indies and England. He was also a president of the Bahamas Cricket Association.

Gene Toote was also flamboyant, although he could not compare to Thompson. Toote was loud, had a great sense of humour, and was a good family man, but he was not in the habit of donating his money to anything. Father Alien, like Munnings, was a quiet character. Most of the time he worked in his own chicken shack on Wulff Road or at his bar on East Street.

I recall when Munnings had a disastrous Saturday. The Cuban draw took place much earlier than usual and punters in Nassau, who had heard the broadcast on Cuban radio, were able to buy the winning number before sales were closed. Percy lost quite a sum of money on that day.

The drawings involved placing numbered balls or marbles into a cloth bag, which was shaken, thrown into the air, and caught. The catcher would hold one of the balls in the bag, which would be tied, and the others released from the bag. The tied ball was the winner. There were rumours that the Numbers houses often removed heavily sold numbers from the bag before it was thrown, but these stories were never connected to Munnings or Thompson, who were both considered trusted operators.

In 1956, CID detectives were looking to arrest a burglary suspect nicknamed Bull-Lizard, and I received information from a local prostitute that he frequented the Corona Club in the early afternoons, so I paid the club a visit for the first time. While there I observed persons buying numbers, and detained two women along with the bar tender, who had sold the numbers. I confiscated the receipts and called CID from a telephone in the bar.

Detective Inspector B. J. Nottage (father of the present National Security Minister) arrived promptly with detectives Courtney Strachan, Reginald Dumont, Albert Miller and Leonard Taylor. We searched the premises using a rapidly acquired warrant and seized a lot of Numbers paraphernalia. Thompson and two employees were prosecuted for breaches of the gaming law. They pleaded guilty and paid their fines.

After this, Wenzel Grainger, a highly respected senior officer, was chosen to form a special team of police officers to address the Numbers racket. In the ensuing weeks, several arrests were made, mostly of vendors for Thompson's operation. We were not picking on Thompson, it was just that his vendors tended to be less discreet than others.

Eventually, it was decided to go after Thompson himself. We observed his bag man collecting money from vendors, which

Wenzel Grainger

he would take to Thompson's Mackey Street residence in the evenings. We planned to arrest "junior" (as the bag man was known) when he arrived with the money ,and then execute a search warrant on Thompson's home. But what actually transpired seemed like a nightmare at the time.

Courtney Strachan was the sergeant in charge of the squad of detectives armed with the search warrant. The remainder of the squad consisted of Sergeants Fletcher Johnson, Lawrence Major and myself. Grainger and his team had worked on the investigation of Thompson in strict secrecy. He apparently had a premonition of danger and so had authorised Strachan to carry a firearm - a loaded .38 revolver with six spare rounds.

On the night of the raid, Junior arrived at the scene with a bag containing records of the number sales from various outlets. We arrested him on the street outside Thompson's two-storey home, but the commotion alerted his boss, who tried to get away. We followed Thompson into his garage, with Strachan holding Junior at the back of his trousers to restrain him, me walking alongside Strachan, while Johnson and Major brought up the rear.

At the rear of the garage was a room with an open door. As we entered the garage I saw Thompson walking towards us from the room with one hand behind his back. He stopped about six feet away and shot Junior, who fell to the floor dead. Then Thompson took aim at a stunned Sergeant Strachan and pulled the trigger - but the gun did not fire. I shouted "shoot, shoot" as we rushed for cover, and Strachan fired a shot in the air. Thompson retreated to the room at the rear of the garage and began shooting at us. The gunfire soon attracted a large crowd on Mackey Street.

Eventually, a squad from the Internal Security Division arrived in the Riot Squad vehicle. They were well-armed, but for some reason remained on the opposite side of Mackey Street and did not enter Thompson's yard, where the action was taking place. Strachan ran over to them and I could hear him shouting at the ISD officers. He then returned to our position just outside the garage door, where we were still under fire.

Suddenly, we were joined by Superintendent Hamish Dougan, an English officer attached to the Criminal Investigation Department, who had arrived on the scene by accident on his way home. Dougan was a combat veteran, having served in the Royal Marines. He was quickly briefed and we pointed out the dead bag man lying at the garage entrance. Dougan sent Lawrence Major to get a tear gas gun and two canisters of gas. He also asked for a loud hailer.

Dougan fired a can of tear gas into the room where Thompson was holed up. When it exploded, Thompson began shouting to his wife that the police were going to kill him. Using the loud hailer, Dougan ordered Thompson to drop his weapons and come out with his hands up. He repeated this instruction three times but the only response from Thompson was "they come to kill me". So Dougan fired the second cannister of gas into the room and Thompson began screaming.

He rushed out of the room with a gun in each hand and hid behind a pillar in the garage. Dougan warned him to drop the weapons and, when he hesitated, the Englishman fired three shots from his revolver, which ricocheted off the pillar near Thompson, who then emerged with his hands up, but still clutching the weapons. After some hesitation, he dropped the guns and we were able to handcuff him.

Playing to the crowd, Thompson began shouting that the police had shot poor Junior down like a dog. The body was taken to the morgue, while we escorted Thompson down to CID, where an intense investigation was launched.

Junior's bag contained cash and records of number sales. The room in the garage contained more records and other numbers paraphernalia. A revolver that had recently been fired was also found in the room. Another gun was found on the floor of the garage, and over 40 rounds of spent ammunition were collected from the scene, as well as the bullet from Junior's body. Thompson was charged with murder and remanded into custody, but we knew he would argue that the police had killed Junior. This was also the story circulating on the streets.

The revolvers used by Strachan and Dougan were secured by the officer in charge of CID, along with all bullets and shell casings which were properly tagged. We contacted the Jamaican police for assistance because at that time we did not have the kind of relationship with the US Federal Bureau of Investigation and other American law enforcement agencies that we enjoy today.

I was chosen to take all of the firearms evidence to Jamaica, where I met Dr. Owen Ellington who took several days to complete his work. Dr. Ellington's report identified the bullets and casings found on the scene that were fired from the various guns. Most

Central Police Station on Bank Lane housed a number of police units over the years, including the Criminal Investigation Department

importantly, he identified the bullet taken from Junior's body as having come from one of the guns used by Thompson.

At the preliminary inquiry, Thompson was represented by three top lawyers - Eugene Dupuch, Gerald Cash and Loran Pyfrom, but the prosecution's evidence was presented with very little cross-examination by any of them. At the trial in the Supreme Court, I was called to testify early so that the exhibits, which were crucial evidence, could be presented and marked.

Cross-examination focused mainly on the identification of the exhibits - firearms, bullets and casings. Knowing the ability of Eugene Dupuch, all detectives involved were well prepared, with pocket-book notes documenting times and stages of the incident. The questioning was intense as Dupuch and Cash tried to poke holes in the evidence, but there were none to be found. I had the distinct privilege of listening to Dr. Ellington when he gave evidence.

He spoke of the test bullets from the police guns and Thompson's guns, and pointed out to the jury the striations that were similar to the striations on the bullets collected at the crime scene. He showed photographs of the area at the rear of bullets that are hit by the striking pin when guns are fired, and demonstrated the similarities between test bullets taken from the guns delivered to him.

The most critical evidence was the fact that the bullet taken from Junior's body came from Thompson's gun, which he identified. Cross-examination by Dupuch followed, with the attorney trying to discredit Ellington, who was a criminologist, chemist, firearms examiner and pathologist with years of experience. Eventually, Dupuch read a paragraph from a book on firearms examination that supported his arguments. But Ellington was able to recite two of the next paragraphs in the book and the attorney took his seat.

The "police shoot poor Junior down like a dog" defence was torn to shreds by this noted expert from Jamaica, and the jury returned in no time with a manslaughter verdict. There was always the possibility that the fatal bullet had been intended for Sergeant Strachan, and the jury may have taken that into consideration. But in the end, Thompson, after an eloquent mercy plea from Gerald Cash, received only a light sentence of imprisonment.

CHAPTER 8

Scotland Yard–the Maxie and Grenidge Murders

The Criminal Investigation Department that I joined in the 1950s was a proud group of well-trained, officers who were dedicated to fighting crime. They were disciplined and determined men who also enjoyed a great sense of humour, which helped to relieve the stress of police work.

The upper ranks of the Department included Bernard Nottage, Salathial Thompson, Albert Miller and Carl Glinton to name a few - there were about 16 in all. At the time there was no fraud squad, no special branch, and no drug squad. We were involved in all types of investigations, on all the islands of the Bahamas, and we also had to provide security for the governor and other top officials.

Our esprit de corps often caused some jealousy amongst the uniformed branches, who believed we had a superiority complex. The publicity we naturally received in the mass media no doubt helped to create this impression.

Salathial Thompson

I worked on teams investigating two key murders during this period. Miss Maxie was an Englishwoman who worked for H. G Christie real estate. Grenidge was a Barbadian of English ancestry who worked in the hotel industry. These were considered high-profile murders in the context of the times, so the governor decided to bring in Scotland Yard detectives to handle the investigations.

This did not sit well with many of us at CID. In fact, we compared it to the Duke of Windsor's decision to bring in American investigators after the murder of Sir Harry Oakes in 1943. I had read the Oakes murder file and heard accounts of the local investigation under Erskine Lindop. Senior officers Herbert Pemberton and Eddie Sears were key witnesses at the trial.

From my limited experience at the time I was convinced that if the local detectives had been allowed to continue their work without interference the Oakes killer would have been found. So I could see why in these later murders many of the older officers grumbled about the arrival of Scotland Yard personnel.

For the Maxie murder, a superintendent named John Bailey led the British team, and he had a reputation as a top murder investigator. At the time I was a detective sergeant and was selected for the investigating team along with Anthony Fields, Fletcher Johnson, Louis Hemmings and Lawrence Major. Bailey exuded self-confidence and it was clear to us from the break that we could learn a lot from this man.

Miss Maxie was in her 40s and lived alone in a two-storey house on Queen Street near the US Embassy. A housekeeper found her body in the bedroom when she arrived at work one morning and ran out screaming into the road while neighbours called the police.

Stanley Moir led the crime scene examination and his thoroughness was a training exercise in itself. When taking notes he would loudly announce whatever it was he was noting so that we could benefit from his experience.

The house had been entered through a broken window on the ground floor and Miss Maxie had been killed in her bed. There were definite signs of a struggle - there were head injuries and marks on her throat. Her clothing was torn, exposing the lower part of her body and it was assumed that she had been raped by her attacker. The room was fingerprinted and searched while photos were taken. No weapon was found, but we came to the conclusion that the assailant had banged Miss Maxie's head against the metal bedstead.

Dr Frederick Duck, the hospital pathologist, visited the scene and inspected the body. He determined that death had occurred after 11pm the previous night and that the victim had indeed been raped.

Since Miss Maxie worked for the Christies, her death sparked rumours that she had been killed to prevent her from revealing what she knew about the Oakes murder.

We began our inquiries by interviewing all the neighbours on Queen Street and the dead women's colleagues at work. By this time Supt Bailey had taken charge and he instructed us to stop and question everyone walking or driving on Marlborough Street, Queen Street and West Hill Street from 10pm to 6am to see if they could recall anything suspicious from the night of the murder. Most of the people we interviewed worked at the nearby British Colonial Hotel.

Meanwhile, the Scotland Yard detectives revisited the crime scene and conducted their own inquiries in the neighbourhood. The boundaries of our night inquiries were widened as we moved into West Street, Virginia Street, Cumberland Street and Nassau Street. We also conducted house to house inquiries during the day.

Early in my career I had learned that to be successful investigators had to develop trust among their informants. I was often able to get people to give me information because they were confident that I would not expose their identity. I also maintained good public relations through my participation in a variety of competitive sports.

While we were investigating the Maxie murder I received a call from a woman who usually walked home along West Hill Street after work late at night. She told me about her encounter with a man loitering at the top of the Queen Street steps on the night before the murder. When the man started to walk towards her she ran away screaming and he did not pursue. On the night of the murder she saw the same man - whom she described as a vagrant - run up Queen Street steps and into Hospital Lane north. I passed this information on to Bailey and he told me to take the Rogues Gallery (our album containing hundreds of photos of known criminals) to her in an unmarked car.

After a while she identified a suspect who had a record for assaults on women, vagrancy and attempted rape. He was eventually located at Sandilands Hospital where he had been remanded for observation after being arrested for throwing missiles at the police. Bailey met with the medical authorities at the hospital and received certain information that convinced him we had the right man. In the absence of any fingerprint evidence he thought that a skillful interrogation might crack the case.

Bailey and another British officer interviewed the suspect at CID, but it was obvious to them that the man was either crazy or playing crazy, so he was turned over to us for another shot. It became clear we were dealing with a lunatic. For example, he told us that his name was Jesus and that he had dropped from a tree. But I observed a change in his demeanour when we asked him about Miss Maxie. He never answered us, so we sent him back to Sandilands.

The next step was to take photos of the suspect to show the neighbours on Queen Street and adjacent streets to see if anyone recognised him. But the effort was fruitless. Eventually Bailey and his team returned to London, disappointed that the Maxie murder was left unsolved. He recommended that the government send Bahamian officers for specialist training in Britain and increase the size of CID.

Some years later a prominent businessman was murdered in a cottage on the corner of Bank Lane and Shirley Street. Edward Grenidge was a Barbadian with an English background who often associated with the political elite of that era. He was a flamboyant social gadfly whom many considered to be gay. He also had some form of relationship with the Christie family.

Grenidge was found by a housekeeper in his home. He had been stabbed multiple times, but there was no evidence of forced entry. Stanley Moir again led the crime scene investigation and we left satisfied that Grenidge had been killed the night before his body was found by someone he knew.

We launched a similar series of inquiries to the ones conducted after the Maxie murder, interviewing people moving along Shirley Street at night who may have noticed something suspicious. We also reconstructed the deceased's movement on the day and night before his death, and closely questioned his circle of friends.

I interviewed the housekeeper who had found him. She told me that a young local man was a frequent visitor at the cottage, but in recent days they had engaged in several arguments over money. She gave me a description and even recalled his first name. Although she reviewed the Rogue's Gallery, the individual in question was not pictured. She agreed that the young man was in an intimate relationship with Grenidge, but did not think he had been in trouble with the police. But a photograph of a young man that we found in the cottage was identified by the housekeeper as the frequent visitor. We immediately launched a search for the suspect.

This time the Scotland Yard team arrived too late. By the time Superintendent Ellicot, who was also a renowned murder investigator, arrived with his men we already had the suspect in custody and ready for arraignment.

The crime scene examination had lifted fingerprints in the cottage that were neither Grenidge's nor the housekeeper's, and we had confirmed that these prints were made by the suspect. Under interrogation the young man had at first denied knowing Grenidge or visiting the cottage, but we knew by then that he was lying. A search of his home turned up a gold watch with Grenidge's initial engraved on the back, which he said he had bought.

In the final interrogation we disclosed all the evidence we had against him and he decided to confess. During an argument at the cottage, the young man said Grenidge had attacked him and he had lost his cool. Grabbing a kitchen knife he had stabbed Grenidge to death and then disposed of the knife in the street on his way home. The maid was given a description of the knife and concluded that it was one of a set that had gone missing.

The Scotland Yard team reviewed the Grenidge file and pronounced their satisfaction with the way the investigation had been conducted before returning to London.

The Maxie murder had dented the pride of CID personnel, but our success in the Grenidge case restored our esprit de corps.

Scotland Yard is the headquarters of the Metropolitan Police Service in London. The name derives from the location of the original police headquarters at Whitehall Place, which had a rear entrance on a street called Great Scotland Yard. The Scotland Yard entrance became the public entrance to the police station, and over time the street and the police became synonymous. The force moved from Scotland Yard in 1890, and the name New Scotland Yard was adopted for the new headquarters. The current New Scotland Yard is in Victoria and has been police headquarters since 1967.

CHAPTER 9

A Roll Call of Police Commissioners

G.H. Ranoe was appointed commissioner in 1949, but he left The Bahamas shortly before my arrival from Trinidad in March 1951. I recall hearing that he had a prosthetic leg.

When I arrived as a young recruit, R. J. Verall had just been appointed commissioner. He was a good administrator who commanded the respect of his men. The junior officers nicknamed him "papa". In those days the commissioner would hear all disciplinary charges brought against police personnel, holding court in his office. These trials were prompt - in some instances on the day of the incident. Verall got his nickname because of his fair and just approach in these disciplinary hearings, and the relatively light sentences he imposed.

In the 1950s gambling was a major disciplinary problem in the police barracks. At the time, John Crawley had just been promoted to sergeant and was working in the barracks when he received information about a card game in a room occupied by a constable named Saunders. Entering the room unaccompanied he saw a group of officers seated on the floor with cards and cash at hand. But before Crawley could open his mouth, Constable Saunders (who was called

John Crawley

Garbo) shouted: "Sir, I was on duty all night and I asked these men to stop gambling so I could sleep."

By this time the officers had gathered up their money, leaving the cards on the floor. Crawley now considered Saunders to be his witness that the other men were gambling, and he marched them off to be dealt with. When Garbo testified at the hearing he responded to Verall's questioning: "Gambling sir? If you look at my file the only disciplinary convictions I have is for gambling. If there was a game in my room you can be sure that I would have been in it." At which point Verall admonished Crawley for wasting his time, and dismissed the case against the officers. But unfortunately for Saunders, from that time on, in whatever division he was posted to, Crawley was his senior officer. He suffered in this way until his transfer to the CID, where he reached the rank of sergeant and performed with distinction.

Meanwhile, Verall lost the nickname "papa" when he sent a policeman to prison for a serious disciplinary offence.

Eddie Sears replaced Verall in 1954 - the first Bahamian appointed to act as Commissioner. He had served in the armed forces during World War 11, reaching the rank of major, but his appointment was short-lived, and the story told by older policemen is that during the investigation of the 1943 Oakes murder Sears had given evidence that he saw the Christie brothers - Harold and Frank - driving east on West Bay Street from Cable Beach (where the murder had occurred). This statement destroyed the alibi that the Christies had reportedly given to investigators. The Christies were prominent members of the ruling power group of the day (known as the Bay Street Boys), which did not appreciate Sears' testimony and so would not confirm his appointment to the post of commissioner. He was a soft-spoken and polite individual, respected by his men, who spearheaded several police sporting teams - including soccer, cricket and table tennis. Sears retired in 1955. There were only two other Bahamian officers serving at that time - Inspector Wenzel Grainger and Inspector Augustus Roberts. Grainger rose to the rank of Deputy Commissioner and Roberts to the rank of Superintendent before their retirement.

J. H. Colchester-Wemyss was commissioner from 1955 to 1963. He was a true visionary, and the significant changes he brought about boosted the morale of the force. Many of his senior officers considered him eccentric, and some considered his initiatives to be impossible to achieve. In fact, there was a sign in his office that read "The impossible we do at once-miracles take longer." He visited all police buildings, recommending some for renovation and others for demolition and replacement, while generally improving working conditions for officers and mandating that all police properties be landscaped. He acquired new British patrol cars, and developed a more sophisticated command centre. The old prison building at East Street was converted into living quarters, a storage area, and administrative offices, and tennis courts and a volleyball court were added to the old prison compound.

It was Colchester-Wemyss who recruited women to the police service for the first time. He also introduced exams for promotions. Later he added a dog section and changed the uniform to a more appropriate bush jacket during the summer. He designed the police flag, and during his tenure more officers were recruited from the British Caribbean. The annual Police Christmas and New Year's banquets that he introduced became a major social activity for the town and helped to lift the social status of the police.

Colchester-Wemyss developed a close relationship with Roy Solomon, a member of the ruling group who was often known as "the commissar". It was thought that the Commissioner's ability to get things done and acquire more resources for the police was due to this important relationship. During his tenure there was a big increase in the number of police officers sent to the UK for training, and all ranks were included.

Prior to his arrival, officers worked 24-hour shifts, from 10 am until 10 the following day, with bunk beds provided in the stations for rest periods. He changed the system to three eight-hour shifts and recruited more men. Colchester-Wemyss replaced the ubiquitous bicycle with police motor scooters. He attended sporting events in support of police teams and played tennis with his senior officers. He demanded loyalty, dedication, integrity and discipline from all of us, and he refused to interfere with police work. I remember him coming to the Criminal Investigation Department on two occasions. The first was after the theft of a huge quantity of jewellery and expensive wristwatches from John Bull - the latest in a series of similar crimes. Stanley Moir was the officer in charge of CID at the time and he received a blistering attack on our performance as detectives. He went into details of the John Bull break-in, obviously briefed by his wife, who was one of the managers. After this outburst he wanted to know what we needed to solve these break-ins, which he considered to be a top priority.

Garth Johnson

I was put in charge of two teams of detectives (including Anthony Fields, Fletcher Johnson, Louis Hemmings, Lincoln Hercules, Egbert Eastmond, Garth Johnson, Willis Bullard and Edward Johnson. The success of this investigation, the arrest of five men and recovery of most of the stolen goods, is recorded in another chapter of this book. And Colchester-Wemyss visited CID again to commend us for the work.

After unsubstantiated attacks were made on his character, Colchester-Wemyss left the Police Service and was replaced by Nigel Morris (from 1963-1968). Morris was one of the most distinguished officers to be appointed Commissioner in The Bahamas. He was an Inspector-General in the UK and his appointment here was considered a reduction in rank. As a result, the government gave him double pay during his period of service.

During this time there were 12 senior British officers attached to the force. All were provided with residences, paid utilities, a car and a valet, plus paid annual vacations to the UK. Except for Wenzel Grainger, Augustus Roberts, Bernard Nottage and Albert Miller, the top executive management of the Bahamian police force was British. Most of these officers had served in the British Army and they helped to improve training and discipline for the local officers.

Morris continued to improve the force and began paying more attention to the out islands, but he was forced to resign in 1968 following a scandal involving the alleged receipt of consultancy fees from the Grand Bahama Port Authority. By this time both Albert Miller and Salathiel Thompson were in a position to lead the force. Thompson was the favourite of Prime Minister Lynden Pindling and his government, although it was well known that Miller was the senior officer and was better trained for the position. The government decided to make them both deputy commissioners, but neither was appointed. Miller was sent to run the Grand Bahama division while Thompson remained in Nassau.

In 1968 another British officer named T. E. Clunie was appointed commissioner, just in time for the opening of the new police headquarters. He was famous for making on-the-spot promotions and was pleasant in his personal relations, but utterly lacking in administrative ability. On one occasion, Prime Minister Pindling called a meeting of senior officers to discuss the lack of morale among police. But despite their frequent criticism of Clunie's administration, most of the men remained silent at the meeting. Edney Johnson and myself were the only two officers who addressed the meeting. I was concerned about neglect of the CID, where the case load was too high and we lacked transportation. Some officers were concerned that we had spoken up about our departmental problems.

Clunie was replaced in 1971 by J. H. Hindmarsh, who was appointed to prepare the police force for independence. It was around this time that Albert Miller retired from the service, which turned out to be a blessing in disguise for him, as he became a leading figure in the Grand Bahama Port Authority.

Before he left the Bahamas, Hindmarsh had arranged training for me at Interpol in France from 1974 to 1975. Upon my return we launched Interpol-Bahamas. By then, Salathiel Thompson had been named Commissioner, and he provided office space and a woman police officer named Sheila Armbrister. In the early years of our careers Thompson and I were close. As a sergeant in the CID who prosecuted cases in court, Thompson provided training in the criminal law and counselled me in investigations. He was the best police prosecutor in the country.

One of the things I admired about Thompson was his outspokenness, even when addressing his superiors. He also looked forward to improving working conditions on the force. In fact, he led the signing of a petition to Commissioner Verall for an increase in the clothing allowance for detectives. The petition had a clause saying if the request was not met CID officers would report for work in uniform. After a long period with no response, Thompson had us all sign applications for uniforms, and soon thereafter we received an increase in our clothing allowance.

I spoke to Thompson often about the role of police associations in other countries in improving working conditions, and he was always interested. While he was still a deputy superintendent, I received word that Pindling wanted Thompson to be the next commissioner and I joked to him about this one day in conversation. Thompson said it would never happen and we made a bet that I eventually won.

But Commissioner Thompson appeared to lose interest in providing better working conditions for the men and women under his command, although he was aware that our conditions were poor compared to other territories in the region. Police received no overtime pay or time back for the excessive hours they worked, nor for attending court on off-duty days or during vacation. There was no group medical insurance, and the death benefit for an officer killed in the line of duty was a year's salary plus the cost of a funeral, rated according to rank.

Once, during the visit of an inspector-general from England, I was asked in the presence of the commissioner and other senior officers if there was anything I wanted to discuss about Police Associations. The inspector-general advised that we consider forming such an association, and after that meeting I had the impression that Thompson deliberately distanced himself from me. Not long after this I was instructed to visit the commissioner's office. Thompson accused me of being disloyal to the police force and the government. I asked him to put it in writing, but he did not respond and I returned to my office, where I locked the door and sat and cried silently.

Over the next few days I consulted with Orville Turnquest and Cyril Fountain, two attorneys who were familiar with my work as a detective. Their advice was to keep the appointment with the commissioner but say nothing. I also received a call from Kendal Isaacs, former solicitor-general, who agreed with the recommendation of Turnquest and Fountain that I should stop pursuing a police association. So I met with the commissioner, but gave no indication or response on the subject of my possible resignation. I recalled the way in which the same commissioner had got Anthony Fields to sign his resignation letter. Fields left the force minus his pension as a result.

In the ensuing weeks and months I heard nothing more from the commissioner. I did hear from two cabinet ministers who assured me that Thompson had invented the story about the government being behind the charge of disloyalty. However, I remained committed to lobbying for better working conditions for police officers and this story is completed later in this book.

In those days I was not Commissioner Thompson's favourite colleague. In addition to his dislike of my support for a police association, he upbraided me for recommending that Criminal Investigation Department officers be removed from security details at the prime minister's residence. "That will never happen," Thompson insisted. But it did happen - after he resigned.

Gerald Bartlett was a great Bahamian gentleman and a respected, compassion-ate and understanding commissioner. He took over leadership of the force when morale was low and in a short time he had moulded it into an effective and vibrant organisation again. Bartlett was able to inspire officers to perform above the call of duty and was regarded as a mixture of the best attributes of Col-chester-Wemyss and Sears. He spoke quietly but firmly, and was always taken seriously. Through his exceptional leadership skills, Bartlett was able to restore team spirit and pride in the police force, and through his care for the men and women under his

Gerald Bartlett

command, he was able to improve living and working conditions. He was the best of all the commissioners up to that time. We just loved the man.

I first met Bartlett as a corporal in the Pay Office when I enlisted. He was always in the forefront of police sporting activities and he especially loved cricket. As an hon-ourary member of the Wanderers cricket club he made significant contributions to the club's overseas tours. I recall going to see him in 1980 as I was about to leave the force. It was Bartlett who advised me to take up the offer from Resorts International, and it was Bartlett who made me deputy commandant of the Police Reserve after my resignation.

CHAPTER 10

Murder of a Haitian Diplomat– Scaling the Wall of Silence

The killing of a young Haitian diplomat in the 1960s generated international publicity. The diplomat had been visiting Freeport, Grand Bahama when he was shot several times in a duplex owned by several Haitian women. He tried to escape his attacker by climbing through a window into the yard, where his body was found. Despite a rapid response by Grand Bahama police, the gunman was not captured.

I led the investigation, as head of the Criminal Investigation Department in Freeport, with my colleague Anthony Fields, who was with CID in Nassau at the time. It was my first exposure to the culture of secrecy among immigrants as we attempted to get information from the multitude of Haitian nationals living in the immediate vicinity of where the crime took place. It was frustrating to interrogate individuals who appeared to support the cause of those who had assassinated the diplomat.

Some time later - in 1967 - another Haitian man was murdered and his body was found in bed in a small house he occupied at Eight Mile Rock. At first, foul play was not suspected, as we could not find any marks of violence or other evidence to suggest he had died from anything other than natural causes. It was a Monday morning and the body was flown to New Providence for autopsy. Later that day I received a telephone call from New Providence informing me that the man was murdered. The pathologist was Dr Joan Reid, an Englishwomen who had held the position at the Princess Margaret Hospital for many years. I was familiar with her work. She was always thorough and provided much information of use to investigators.

Her report said that a .32 calibre bullet had entered the deceased's body through his left armpit and lodged in his lung. The man had been bleeding internally for two or three days before he died. The entry wound was difficult to spot, which was why we had concluded there were no signs of violence at the initial examination.

The body had been found by Bahamian neighbours on Monday morning, who said they had not seen the man for the entire weekend. When they entered the house through an open door looking for him, they found him dead on the bed. Inquiries in the neighbourhood revealed that the deceased had gone to a Haitian dance on Friday night with two male friends. As they were walking home from the event a car drove up and the driver began shooting at them. They all escaped and got home safely, but the deceased began complaining of not feeling well. He had been drinking heavily that night so they put him to bed and left for their own homes.

We tried to find a motive for the drive-by shooting incident and learned there were two big social events on that Friday night, both of which were well-attended by Haitians. The other event was a gambling marathon in a building on the same road where the shooting took place. It took us weeks of interviews to establish the facts about the dance event - the owner consistently denied that any such event had taken place on his property, even when we presented him with the musicians who had played at the dance. We wanted to find out if there had been any altercations that could have led to the drive-by shooting.

I knew a Haitian prostitute who lived in the area and she helped me conduct some of the interviews with the gamblers, but the fabrications and denials were very frustrating. It turned out that most of the people we interviewed had work permits so I asked Garnet Levarity at the Immigration Department for help. We called in all the Haitians we had been interviewing to the Department where Levarity told them that if they refused to co-operate their permits would be revoked. That was the only way we were able to get statements from those who had information on the case, and after several months we were able to put together a summary of what had happened that Friday night.

There was a dice game in a building just west of where the dance was held. A Bahamian with a criminal record named Kendal Pinder (also known as Cory X) had joined the game. I knew him well, as he had threatened me on several occasions. At some point in the game Cory X had managed to switch the dice and proceeded to win big time. Then a well-dressed Haitian who worked on a cruise ship joined the game, but left soon after becoming suspicious about the dice. Cory X, nervous about being discovered, blew out the candles, grabbed the money on the floor and ran. But he was pursued by the other players, caught and severely beaten. He was left cursing and threatening revenge on his attackers.

My prostitute friend also knew Cory X and said he would often drink for hours at a bar in Eight Mile Rock. One of our detectives, Ormond Briggs, knew the owner of this bar well and was able to discover that Cory X had visited the bar that Friday night dishevelled and bruised. He borrowed the proprietor's car ostensibly to drive himself to hospital, and returned it an hour later. From the description it appeared to be the same car used in the drive-by shooting. We decided to take Cory X in for questioning, but he was nowhere to be found on the island. In fact, weeks went by and we were unable to locate him anywhere in the Bahamas.

One day in the office we were talking about our failure to capture this man and a detective who had just returned from vacation said he had seen the fugitive boarding an Air Jamaica flight for Kingston. We soon confirmed that Cory X was in the country, because his weakness for gambling had led to his arrest during a police raid. I was delegated to visit Jamaica and bring him back to Nassau, where he was charged with the murder of the Haitian man in Eight Mile Rock. But defence attorney Kendal Nottage managed to get him acquitted by focusing on the inconsistency of some of the statements of Haitian witnesses. Kendal (Cory X) Pinder was charged with murder twice and acquitted both times. Many years after this experience he begged me for money on Bay Street.

Our investigation of the murder of the Haitian diplomat met with a similar wall of silence among the women he had been visiting on the night of his death. The investigation dragged on for months while Haitian exile radio stations in the US commended the assassin for their achievement.

We had McDonald Chase - a fingerprint expert who spoke Creole fluently - monitor what was said on those radio stations, and eventually we learned of a political group based on Grand Bahama that was planning an invasion of Haiti. Some Haitians on the island were supplying food and water for the guerillas who were training in the bush and although we were able to block this supply chain, they would not reveal the location of the camp to us.

Not long after this, the US Coast Guard notified us that a stolen boat had been found adrift in the Gulf of Mexico with 12 Haitian men on board. The boat had been stolen in Freeport but had run out of fuel, and among those on board was a man named Magloire, who was the relative of a former Haitian president.

Magloire had been employed as an accountant in Freeport and I had met him once or twice. Also in the group was a Haitian medical student from Montreal as well as other well-educated and prominent men. There were no guns on the boat but we did find a few rounds of ammunition similar in calibre to the bullets that killed the diplomat.

From our interrogation of these men, and other circumstantial evidence, we were able to locate the training camp in East Grand Bahama and eventually charged six of them with the assassination. A jury convicted them of manslaughter, but the Privy Council quashed the conviction on appeal. They were held in the Bahamas until other countries were found to take them in. I recall our team being commended by the commissioner for our work in this case, and I also recall Stanley Moir telling me that the president of Haiti had invited us to visit in order to receive his commendations. We all declined the invitation.

CHAPTER 11

Whale Point Murder–
The Case of the Stink Sock

It was a chilly morning on the 12th of December in 1965 when I was summoned to Police Headquarters. I accompanied Stanley Moir, superintendent of the Criminal Investigation Department where I had been posted since 1952.

On that morning, detectives were talking about the Christmas holidays, patrolling the city, preparing for the Junkanoo parades, and other job-related matters. There was also conversation about off-duty entertainment and the annual Christmas party.

Moir and I met with the commissioner in the conference room, along with other senior officers and Sir Sidney Oakes, a son of the late Sir Harry Oakes who was a police reservist and well-known businessman. We were briefed on the murder of Mrs. Janis Catherine Wilburn, which had occurred the previous night at Whale Point, Eleuthera.

I was assigned to investigate with a team of detectives. Sir Sidney had a chartered plane waiting at the airport. My team included McDonald Chase, who the FBI regarded as one of the best fingerprint experts in the region; Anthony Fields; Fletcher Johnson; Louis Hemmings; Lawrence Major and Kemuel Hepburn. I also recruited Dr. Duck, the pathologist at Princess Margaret Hospital. We moved swiftly and were airborne an hour after the briefing.

Kemuel Hepburn

Whale Point is just a few miles from the settlement of Hatchet Bay in central Eleuthera. Inspector Chilean Turner, who was in charge of the district, also joined our team. A resort was under construction at Whale Point by an American firm called International Developers Ltd. Several cottages on the site were occupied by the company's overseas employees, and there was a cafeteria for local and foreign employees. John Wilburn, husband of the deceased, was in charge of the construction project.

We were taken to the murder scene, a cottage at the end of the single road where a maid had run into the street screaming after discovering the body. We saw the dead woman lying on her back in the nude on the bed. There was a huge blood clot on her neck under her chin and marks about her body. There was blood all over the body, the bed and the floor. A trail of blood led to the bathroom, and there was blood in the bath tub.

It was noted by all of us that the late Mrs Wilburn must have been a very beautiful woman. I later learned that she was Hawaiian-American and was formerly a stewardess on a cruise ship. Photos in the cottage confirmed our view on her beauty. It was a very emotional moment as we took in the crime scene. Detective Fields, who we nicknamed "Dog", was very quiet and sad. When I spoke to him he sounded upset by the horror of it all. Dr. Duck began his examination of the body while Detective Chase took photos and dusted for fingerprints. Fields and Hemmings joined me in a thorough search of the cottage.

Chase and Dr. Duck returned to Nassau with the body. Some fingerprint smudges were found, but not enough for identification. The most important information came from Dr. Duck, who confirmed that the deceased had been raped after death. There was no evidence of forced entry at the cottage, and while we searched the scene of the crime other detectives were interviewing residents and employees at the resort. We learned that on the night of the murder all of the residents, except the deceased and two elderly American men, had gone to the cinema at Hatchet Bay to see a double feature.

The husband of the deceased helped to identify items found to be out of place in the cottage. And Fields, in searching the bathroom, found a sock, which Wilburn said did

The 300-acre Whale Point Club resort was built by Sir Sydney Oakes and opened in the mid-1960s. Sydney's father, Sir Harry Oakes, had been murdered in Nassau in 1943. Sydney's brother, William, died at the age of 27 of a sudden illness in New York. And Sydney himself died in a single-car accident in Nassau in 1966, only a few months after the resort opened. A long succession of future owners could not manage to keep the resort open for more than a few months. The resort featured a clubhouse, two blocks of rooms, several cottages, a restaurant, swimming pool, and marina. Of the original cottages, only two survive today as private homes. Little remains of the others, including the murder site.

not belong to him. The sock was very dirty and a part of the sole was hard. It was also very stink. Fields remarked to me "we have to find the other side of this sock or the feet that wore it." He was referring to the smell.

We worked very into the evening conducting inquiries at Hatchet Bay and the local police set up road blocks on the road between Hatchet Bay and Whale Point to question drivers of any vehicles seen entering or leaving the resort. Late that night we met to discuss progress and plan for the next day. The detectives were dispirited because all their hard work seemed to have been in vain. We reviewed the little information that seemed to be of value.

First, the two elderly men who did not attend the movies were in their apartment when they heard a vehicle moving on the street, with no engine on. They also heard a door in the area near to their apartment open and close twice during the evening. They were both in bed at the time and did not try to investigate.

Second, the stink sock found in the bathroom suggested that the murderer had bathed himself after the killing and rape, inadvertently dropping one sock when leaving the premises.

Third, the amount of sand found on the cottage floor indicated that the murderer walked along the beach to get to the house and his shoes carried sand into the house.

Fourth, the fact that there was no sign of forced entry and that the back door to the beach was the only open entrance confirmed that the victim either went to bed with the door unlocked, or she had opened the door for someone she knew. Her husband convinced us that his wife was very security conscious and would not have left the door unlocked. He also said the back door was hardly ever used.

We all believed that the murderer was a foreigner because we could not see a Bahamian raping a woman after death. We had confirmed through the FBI that Wilburn had been in Florida on the night of his wife's murder, but the local policeman told us that a young white man who worked at the resort appeared to be very interested in the progress of the investigation.

It was a miserable night for most of us, due both to our lack of progress and to Detective Fields' whistling snores, which made sleep near impossible in the open dormitory that we bunked in.

On the following day one of the detectives prayed for God's guidance. We proceeded to the cafeteria for breakfast when Fields said a kitchen worker wanted to see me. She was an elderly woman from Nassau who spoke to me outside about a young white man who ate all of his meals in the cafeteria. He usually sat in a corner by himself and could not take his eyes off Janis Wilburn as she moved around the cafeteria. She was certain that the man she described had something to do with her death. The victim was in charge of the cafeteria and was usually there helping with the service.

We made discreet inquiries about the young man and learned that Frederick McConville lived alone in the apartment below the one occupied by the two elderly Americans. He was employed in the field of explosives and heavy equipment. We immediately obtained a search warrant, picked him up as a suspect and proceeded to his apartment where Detective Fields immediately searched the laundry hamper and identified the smell of the stink sock. A search for bloodstained clothing turned up nothing, but we knew we were on target and that it was important to skilfully interrogate the suspect as soon as possible.

I took on the task, trying to impress the suspect that we had evidence which pointed to him. We used the sock that was left in the bathroom. We talked about the sand in the house, the blood in the bathroom, and the noise from the car and the opening and closing of doors heard by the two elderly men upstairs. We told him that we knew that he had left the cinema in Hatchet Bay and I could see he was getting nervous. By this time we had received an album of photographs taken at the scene and in the mortuary by McDonald Chase. The horror depicted in these photographs brought tears to his eyes and a full confession.

McConville had worked on the same cruise ship as Janis Wilburn had. He admired her beauty and fell in love with her, but she never encouraged any intimate relationship with him, although they maintained a casual friendship. In 1965 she and her husband John were in Miami on business and were on Flagler Street shopping when she saw McConville for the first time in months. She introduced him to her husband, who offered him a job at Whale Point, which he accepted. He started work there on December 6, 1965. He continued to see her Janis on the road and in the cafeteria where she worked, and when her husband was away and the other residents were at the Hatchet Bay cinema he decided to confront her.

After driving to the movie theatre, he left quietly during the showing and returned to Whale Point. He cut off the engine at enough speed to keep the car moving quietly and stopped near the cottage. He went to the back door, which was locked, and called out for Janis, asking her for some headache pills. She let him in and went to get the pills, but he could not restrain himself from grabbing her. At the time she was in her sleeping clothes. When she resisted his attack, he threw her on the bed and to stop the resistance he used his knife to cut her throat. Blood gushed onto the bed and onto his clothing and McConville soon realized that Janis was dead. But he had to get what he went there for so he raped her anyway.

Afterwards he went to the bathroom, removed his shoes and socks, and showered still wearing the bloodied clothing. He collected his shoes, inadvertently leaving one sock on the floor of the bathroom, and left through the back door for his apartment, where he changed into dry clothing. He took the wet clothing and shoes to his car, gave it a push, and rolled it away from the apartments. He dumped the clothes off the Glass Window Bridge and then drove back to the theatre where he remained until the end of the movies, returning to Whale Point with the other residents.

During my interrogation and the recording of his statement he continued to show great remorse and the tears flowed from him. At the trial an American psychiatrist testified in his defense, confirming that McConville had been detained in a state mental hospital for a similar criminal act. It was also disclosed that he had a poor record in the US Army from where he was dishonourably discharged. McConville was imprisoned for life and subsequently removed to serve his time in the US. Unfortunately, his victim, Janis Catherine Wilburn, had been pregnant with her first child at the time of her death.

CHAPTER 12

The Police Staff Association

The idea of a Police Staff Association in The Bahamas existed as far back as the late 1950s. As a detective, I visited the Trinidad and Tobago Police Service and the Jamaica Constabulary on official business several times and learned that the conditions of service in those countries was much better than in the Bahamas.

In conversation with officers in those countries I learned that staff associations had been able to achieve a great deal not only in conditions of service but in the delivery of service to the public. Over the years I obtained lots of literature on police staff associations from officers throughout the British Commonwealth, as well as the United States.

In many of these countries the staff associations were consulted by senior officers on administrative matters such as uniforms, vehicles, crime prevention measures and training. In this way, information from the lowest ranks of the organisation was available to the top executive. It was also notable that the executive officers, including the commissioner, were members of the association.

In most cases there were two divisions in each association - one for the lower ranks and one for those above the rank of inspector. My early discussions on this subject were confined to close friends and colleagues, mainly in the Criminal Investigation Department. As I progressed in rank I broadened the group of officers with whom I discussed this subject, and also circulated literature I had received from my international police contacts, including newsletters and magazines.

In the early years one of my confidants was Salathial Thompson, whom I considered a mentor. Initially he was very encouraging and willing to debate the merits of a staff association in The Bahamas. By 1970 I was acting as an assistant commissioner while Thompson had reached the rank of deputy commissioner and it became clear to me that his enthusiasm for such an initiative had waned. There were others whose interest had likewise diminished. Eventually I learned from Thompson that the government was opposed to a staff association.

However, many lower ranking officers were still committed to the idea and we proceeded to lobby for political support. Our interest was sparked by the comparison between conditions of service in The Bahamas and in other Commonwealth countries.

CHAPTER 206

ROYAL BAHAMAS POLICE STAFF ASSOCIATION

An Act to establish the Royal Bahamas Police Staff *7 of 1997*
**Association, to make provision for the formation,
constitution and functions of such an association and
provision in respect of matters connected thereto.**

[Commencement 6th February, 1997]

1.   This Act may be cited as the Royal Bahamas Police   Short title
Staff Association Act, 1997.

For example, most Bahamian officers worked a 12-hour day at least six days a week. In the CID we worked a 12-hour day seven days a week, with no overtime pay or time back. In addition, many officers had to attend court during their off-duty time. Very often, when there was an increase in crime or a special event or VIP visit, police officers were put on 12-hour shifts and willingly performed their duties. But we knew that other police services received overtime pay or time back arrangements.

Death benefits were another bone of contention. There was no insurance for police officers in The Bahamas. The surviving spouse received one year's wages plus a burial fee. If the funeral expenses were greater than the allotted fee they were deducted from the year's wages. The arrangement was the same for a police officer killed in the course of duty. In some countries the spouse would receive part wages up to a certain period and the children's school fees would be covered, particularly in cases where the officer had died on duty.

The promotions board in The Bahamas consisted of a deputy commissioner and the assistant commissioners. The deliberation process was usually fair, but it could be abused by senior personnel. Some officers were excluded from consideration by their commanding officers due to personal conflicts. In such cases, the recommending officers had to show why officers who were senior in service were being bypassed, and their excuses were often fabrications. One particular commissioner gave the promotions board a list of ranks to be filled which would be less than the number actually required. This was his way of ensuring that the officers he wanted to promote were taken care of. If his choices were not recommended by the board, he would add them to the list. And he frequently struck off persons who were recommended by the board. I even heard him say that as long as he was commissioner certain officers would never be promoted.

On one occasion Assistant Commissioner Courtney Strachan had the courage to question the commissioner's deletion of a female officer from Special Branch who had been recommended for promotion by the board. The board resisted this action and the commissioner subsequently agreed, but recommended her immediate transfer, which was a form of punishment. A similar case involved one of the commissioner's "home-boys", whose name was deleted on more than one occasion from board recommenda-tions. We were able to change his mind in this case too, but he insisted on transferring the officer from CID, where he had served for years with distinction. Both of these officers made it into the senior ranks after this commissioner had resigned.

I can report that the promotions process was significantly improved over the years. Candidates are now interviewed by the board and have the opportunity to challenge any adverse comments made about them by senior officers.

Housing for police officers was another area that stood to be improved. In 1956, he United Bahamian Party government brought in 12 senior officers from the United Kingdom as executives and divisional commanders. These officers were provided with cottages at the police barracks and an adjacent estate called Elizabeth Gardens, where two-storey homes were built. They were provided with vehicles, paid utilities, and tele-phones, as well as a constable to act as a batman - shining their shoes and diving their children to school, etc. These British officers also received paid vacations back to the UK. In the late 60s, when the Progressive Liberal Party took over the government, the British officers were gradually replaced with local officers moving up the ranks. However, these local officers had to rent the cottages, pay all utilities, and were charged a vehicle fee. This was most certainly a form of discrimination. In Jamaica, through the efforts of the police staff association, all of the benefits given to British officers were received by the local officers who replaced them.

Arbitrary transfers have always been an issue in the public service. Very often when officers are posted to the family islands, no consideration was given to individual circum-stances. For example, a policeman's wife could have a good job in Nassau that covered their mortgage payments, but that job would not be available to her on another island. Or an officer could be receiving medical treatment in the capital that would be unavail-able in the out islands. I remember one deputy commissioner who liked to tell officers being transferred that their families were not members of the police force.

There was also the unfortunate case of a detective corporal in Freeport who was doing an exceptional job monitoring drug offenders in that community. Unfortunately for him he arrested a group of youths in possession of marijuana at a basketball court. Their parents were high profile individuals with major political contacts. At the time I was charge of the CID on Grand Bahama, and some weeks after the arrest I was notified by the then assistant commissioner-crime that the corporal was to be transferred to Nas-sau. I debated this order with my boss, based on the corporal's outstanding performance in the area of drug arrests. I gave statistics and noted that the corporal's wife was an assistant manager at a Freeport bank with no branches in Nassau, and that they had just acquired a mortgage on a new house. The ACP showed no concern and the corporal was transferred to Nassau. His wife remained in Freeport.

I was later transferred back to Nassau where I met the corporal, who appeared to be very unhappy. He eventually stopped coming to work and was subsequently dis-missed from the force. After that his life took a downward turn when he got involved with a serving police officer in the kidnapping of a bank manager's daughter. I was sent to Freeport with an investigative team, and he and the serving officer were both arrested and convicted for the crime, serving time in prison.

Police officers over the years have been used and abused, not only by their commanding officers, but by politicians and persons of influence and power in the community. In the days of British commanders, police had to protect the homes of wealthy individuals when the adults were out at night. I once spent an evening babysitting two young boys on Paradise Island, which I had to reach by dinghy since there was no bridge at that time. This form of abuse continued throughout the 1960s and 70s, when officers working in the homes of certain government ministers could not use the toilets or get water to drink. Officers were also taken to the farm to help with the harvest. There was very little respect for the police in those days and it is still not what it ought to be.

On one occasion a police officer was transferred to the Fire Department because he arrested a UBP member of parliament for parking in the middle of Bay Street. The MP had refused to show the officer his driver's licence or give his name and address. Another officer was on traffic duty at the corner of Bay Street and Victoria Avenue when he was attacked by the son of a member of parliament for delaying one of his trucks. The man was arrested, but that officer was also subsequently transferred to the Fire Department.

I recall when the late Superintendent Anthony Fields was transferred from Inagua to Nassau. He was accused by a candidate of campaigning for the PLP in an election. In a later year he was suddenly transferred from Freeport to Nassau as staff officer, a position held by sergeants and inspectors. He protested, but the commissioner at the time said he had nowhere else to post him. Unfortunately this led Fields to resign from the force, just a few years before he became pensionable.

In the late 1970s our lobbying for a police staff association threatened my own position on the police force. The commissioner accused me of disloyalty to the government and asked for my resignation. He told me that if I resigned he had the assurance of the then prime minister that I would receive all of my benefits. He gave me a week to decide.

In the meantime I had taken legal advice, and when I reported to the commissioner's office at the end of the week I said nothing, as advised by my attorneys. I was sent back to work, and heard nothing more from him. In fact, he resigned before I left the service. I later heard from two government ministers that the story about my loyalty being in question had been invented by the commissioner, who simply wanted to get rid of me.

After a career of 30 years I resigned from the police service in January of 1981, but I continued to lobby and write to the media about the need for a police association.

The opposition Free National Movement included this commitment in their election platform and when the party was elected in 1992, Cornelius Smith was appointed National Security Minister. I knew Smith well from when he was a Customs officer and we had worked together on investigations. I kept pestering him about a staff Association for the police and eventually one was established in February 1997. However, what was approved by the government was not what was desired. There is no association for police personnel above the rank of inspector, which is not in keeping with other associations in the Commonwealth and in CARICOM.

Paul Farquharson was commissioner when the staff association was formed and he gave it his full support, having been one of those who had endorsed the idea before reaching the executive ranks.

Paul Farquharson

The objectives of the association are "to consider and bring to the notice of the commissioner of police matters affecting welfare and efficiency, including pay, pensions and conditions of service, other than relating to discipline and promotion affecting individual members of the force". Among other things, the association has the authority to seek redress for or settlement of grievances, to evaluate the system of promotions, and to pursue fair labour standards for police officers.

The association is not a labour union and must not participate in union marches, or other similar activities. It must not engage in public communications through the media or by meeting with politicians other than the Minister of National Security. And it must not retain the services of any attorneys involved in politics. The association is required to take its problems, issues and complaints to the commissioner, the minister or other recognised authorities such as the industrial tribunal. Since its establishment in June 1998 the association's achievements have been considerable.

For example, police officers were covered with group medical insurance, received improved death benefits, and a dependants' trust fund was set up for the wives and children of officers killed in the line of duty. There were also changes to the promotions process and consideration of overtime pay or time back for extra hours worked.

CHAPTER 13

A Child's Kidnapping

I consider the kidnapping of a child to be a crime crueler than murder or rape. In the case of murder, families know that death had occurred. With kidnapping, the uncertainty of what is happening to a loved and defenceless child can be particularly painful.

I had read about the Lindburgh baby kidnapping of 1932, in which the dead child was eventually found buried in a shallow grave. It became known as the crime of century in the United States, and my hero, J. Edgar Hoover, was closely involved in the investigation. In The Bahamas, thankfully, kidnapping is not a crime that occurs with any frequency, but in my experience it has occurred at least twice.

In February 1973, in the midst of our preparations for the grand celebration of national independence, we were shocked to learn that a five-year-old girl had been abducted from her well-to-do home in Freeport, Grand Bahama. Residents were outraged and hungered for the arrest of the culprits. Many became concerned for their own children's safety.

Assistant Commissioner John Crawley instructed me to lead a team of detectives to Freeport to supplement the staff of the Criminal Investigation Unit there. Among the officers I selected were Anthony Fields, Edney Johnson, Charles Edwards, Louis Hemmings and police dog Charlie. Crawley accompanied us to Freeport, and I knew that we also had capable officers under Ormond Briggs in the CID Unit there. I was confident we would be able to find the child, but unsure whether she would be alive or not.

Upon our arrival we met a lot of police activity in progress. The public had formed search parties and many had left their vehicles at the Mobile Division for use by police if needed. Ormond Briggs briefed us on the details of the kidnapping. Two masked bandits armed with a shotgun had entered the home of Brandon Spencer, manager of the Royal Bank of Canada branch in Freeport. Spencer lived with his wife in an upscale residential area called "The Ridge" in East Freeport. The intruders held the Spencers at bay and drove off with their five-year-old daughter in the couple's own car, later found abandoned in a wooded area.

We quickly arranged for a police officer to be at the Spencer home to monitor any incoming calls. Grafton Ifill, who was posted in the Grand Bahama Division at the time, was given the job of police public relations officer, while I placed an urgent call to the FBI headquarters in Miami and arranged for a light aircraft if needed as well as vehicle tracking devices and equipment for recording telephone conversations. The equipment was sent with a pilot on an airliner leaving Miami for Freeport. It was police cooperation at its best, with minimal red tape. Meanwhile, the telephone company was enlisted to trace any calls to the Spencer's residence. It was apparent to me when we arrived in Freeport, that the kidnappers would have been aware, that the police was aware of the crime, due to the amount of police/public activity taking

Grafton Ifill

place. We tried to downplay our role as investigators. The situation made me worry even more about the safety of the child.

I interviewed the Spencers in a very sorrowful atmosphere. The household was in tears over the safety of their little girl. I made every effort to reassure them, but up to that point no-one had heard from the kidnappers. Spencer told me about his altercation with the shorter man who was carrying the shotgun. As his daughter was being removed from the house, Spencer punched the intruder on the right jaw, whereupon the gunman fired into the air, which stopped any further attack. Spencer was wearing a large ring on his right finger and it was clear he had broken the skin on the bandit's jaw. We also found a used 12-gauge shotgun cartridge on the floor - a critical piece of evidence.

In the hours that followed, we were able to have some technical aids in place to assist in gathering evidence and tracking the movements of the bank manager. Spencer was receiving calls from various people, including the kidnappers. We were able to trace the kidnappers' calls to pay phones near the Holiday Inn and East Sunrise Highway. They demanded a ransom of $500,000 in cash, and left instructions on how to deliver the ransom in a phone booth. The ransom note was written in block letters. All of the telephone calls were monitored by police officers.

After each call, the officer stationed at the Spencers' home would relay the details to me back at CID headquarters. Incredibly, he seemed to recognize the voice, but could not attach a name to it immediately.

To receive the ransom, the kidnappers had selected an area opposite the Bahamas Cement Factory on the road out of Freeport to Eight Mile Rock. The area is a low-lying pine barren intersected by dirt roads. We were able to track Spencer's car electronically as he delivered the ransom, while Ormond Briggs conducted physical surveillance at a safe distance in an unmarked car. At some time during the operation we noticed some changes in Spencer's mood. He may have been willing to deal with the kidnappers, without our knowledge. I sympathized with him in the knowledge that we could not be sure his daughter would be returned alive even if he did pay the ransom.

A tracking device had been placed in the bag containing the ransom money and we knew where the bag was to be deposited in the pine barren. But on the way, Spencer drove to the King's Inn Resort and switched cars with a friend before continuing his journey. But we were able to follow him by means of the tracking device in the bag. After the bag had been deposited we had to be in place very quickly to observe anyone who came to collect it. We parked at the cement factory and walked through the bush to the bag location within minutes of the drop-off. I was accompanied by Edney Johnson, armed with a sub-machine gun; Briggs, armed with a revolver; Charles Edwards and police dog Charlie.

There was a huge rock with shrubbery growing high around it near the drop-off site where we decided to hide and wait. It was a very cold winter night and we were standing in muddy water in light clothing. There could be no talking, smoking, sneezing or coughing. It was so cold that even the police dog, Charlie, was shivering. After standing there for about seven hours, Crawley back at headquarters decided to call off the stakeout at about 5am. We were unaware of this decision so when we saw headlights lights approaching we prepared to strike.

But instead of the kidnappers, a police constable got out of the car with his hands in the air and began calling to us. He relayed Crawley's instructions and we collected the bag with the money and returned to base. Spencer was informed that the ransom had not been collected, which naturally made him more upset and concerned about the survival of his daughter. The entire Freeport community was incensed over this heinous crime, fearing it could be the start of a wave of terror in wealthy communities. As police officers we were disappointed that we had nothing tangible to go on. Crawley returned to Nassau, leaving me in charge of the investigation, but no further calls were received from the kidnappers. The big question remained - where was the little girl?

The next day something happened that surprised us all, in particular the Spencers themselves. An airline pilot and two stewardesses, who had just arrived on a flight from the US, rented a car and went to the Pineridge pine barren in search of wood roses. They knew the area from previous collection visits, and as they drove through the forest they were startled to see a little girl in the bush. Recalling news stories about a child's kidnapping they stopped and picked the little girl up. Amazingly, the five-year-old was able to direct them to her home several miles away, where she told us about her ordeal.

After being abducted she had been taken to an area in the forest where she was tied up and placed under the floor of an abandoned church. She spent the night there alone and in the dark, saying her prayers as she had been taught by her parents. She worked at the ropes tying her throughout the night until she was able to get loose. And her constant thought was - when would the bad men return?

This five-year-old child was able to give a good description of the two men who had abducted her. She told us they had promised to release her soon and that she must not be scared, but she had cried all night while alone in the church. One tip she gave us was that the men spoke with different accents, but she was convinced one accent was local. I led a team of investigators to the old church where we failed to find anything that could identify the kidnappers.

Back at CID headquarters on Peel Street, we met to review all the available information. Briggs, who had a photographic memory, was re-reading the ransom note when he noticed the word "proceed" had been misspelled as "procede". Briggs recalled a retired police officer named Leroy McLain who had used the same misspelling when writing reports. And at this point, the officer who earlier believed he had recognized the kidnapper's voice on the telephone stood up and shouted: "That's him! It's McLain's voice I heard". Other detectives in the room recalled seeing McLain with a serving officer named Edward Dames together in a car on the day of the kidnapping. And we were able to develop the fact that Dames and McLain were close friends.

I named both men as persons of interest in the case and we set about trying to locate them discreetly. Search warrants were prepared and signed by a magistrate, who allowed us to retain his own copy for the sake of confidentiality. I led a team of detectives to Dames' apartment. When he opened the door, I noticed a bruise on his right jaw and there was a shotgun leaning against the wall.

Dames was told about the crime we were investigating and when I asked him about the bruise on his jaw he told me that he hit himself with a golf club while playing golf. I asked when was the last time he had fired the shotgun and he said several months ago. The shotgun was a 12-guage automatic similar to the one seen at the scene of the crime, and there was powder residue in the barrel indicating that it had been recently fired. Dames was taken into custody and an officer was sent to the FBI lab in Washington with the shotgun and the spent cartridge collected at the scene.

Meanwhile, the search for McLain continued. It was apparent that he had heard of Dames' arrest and was making himself scarce. He was the director of security at a hotel in the Mall opposite the King's Inn Resort and was not in office for a long period of the day. Eventually, he was picked up after an all points bulletin and brought to CID, where we interrogated both men. They denied the accusations, but the FBI lab in Washington quickly identified the shotgun as the one from which the cartridge found at the scene had been discharged. But McLain and Dames continued to deny involvement and we realised that we could not expect a confession as they were police officers who knew that we had to have evidence.

Both men refused to provide us with voice specimens for comparison with the recordings made of the phone calls to the Spencer home. But other police officers who had worked closely with McLain were able to identify his voice and the slight accent he had developed from spending time in schools in Jamaica. We also had the evidence of officers who had seen the two men together in a car near the Spencer home at the crucial time of the kidnapping, and we had the evidence of the Spencers themselves, who identified both suspects. The misspelling on the ransom note only added to the list of circumstantial evidence against McLain. And McLain's verbal statement accounting for his whereabouts at the time of the kidnapping was soon contradicted by personnel in his office and by the diary kept. We were convinced that we had the right men, and both were eventually charged and convicted in the Supreme Court, and sentenced to seven years imprisonment.

Dames worked in the uniform branch and was not well known to me. But I was very familiar with McLain's work in the Criminal Investigation Department in Freeport. I had assigned him to be in charge of the two-man drug unit we had set up and he did a remarkable job. He arrested many young drug users during his time, some from prominent Freeport families. The families constantly complained about the arrests, both to the police in Freeport and in Nassau. They even levelled accusations of police brutality in the hope that this would get their complaints some attention. It did get the attention of Assistant Commissioner John Crawley, who wanted McLain to be transferred to Nassau. I was rebuked when I protested this transfer of a very effective officer whose wife had a good job in Freeport, but the transfer went through.

McLain's wife could not find a similar job in Nassau and between them they could not meet the mortgage payments on their Freeport home. So McLain started missing days from work and was eventually dismissed from the force and returned to Freeport. His transfer to Nassau was most unfair and caused a major change in life.

CHAPTER 14

The Police after Independence

"The concept of justice and the system to adjudicate against the violation of canons law are the foundation stones of progressive civilianization. Right from the ancient tribal societies to the present-day's complex social organism, the keepers of the peace, that is the police, have played a crucial role in maintaining peace and orderliness in society... The rights and duties, accountability and privileges, strength and weaponry, all depended upon the imagination of the particular community, but universally this institution was created to bring peace and orderliness in society." -- R. C. Dikshit, at the 66th general assembly of Interpol

I clearly recall the teaching in British police colleges that I attended during my career. Sir Robert Peel's *Principles of Policing* were constantly drummed into us, and rightly so.

Peel was British prime minister in the 1830s and 40s. Before that, when he was home secretary, he established the London Metropolitan Police and greatly reformed the criminal law, reducing the number of crimes punishable by death. From the 1820s onward, British police officers were nicknamed "bobbies" or "peelers" in his honour.

Sir Robert Peel

Peel was the first to discuss the basic principles of modern policing, and these ideas were gradually codified over the years. They start from the premise that the basic mission of a police force is to prevent crime and disorder as an alternative to military repression. Peel recognized that the ability of the police to perform their duties would always be dependant on public approval. As a result, the police had to secure the willing cooperation of the public in voluntary observation of the law. And the degree of public co-operation was directly inverse to the degree of coercion used to achieve police objectives. Hence, Peel's most often quoted principle: "The police are the public and the public are the police."

The key principle is that the police must preserve public favour, not by catering to public opinion, but by constantly demonstrating impartial application of the law, in complete independence of policy, by ready offering of individual service and friendship to all members of the society without regard to their race and social standing, and by ready offering of individual sacrifice in protecting and preserving life.

The use of physical force to secure observance of the law or to restore order should only occur when the exercise of persuasion, advice and warning is found to be insufficient and only the minimum degree of physical force should be used.

The police should always direct their actions towards their functions and never appear to usurp the powers of the judiciary by avenging individuals or the state, or seeking to judge guilt or punish the guilty. In fact, the test of police efficiency is the absence of crime and disorder, not the visible evidence of police action in dealing with them.

These are the principles that many of us lived with in performing our duties as police officers. Those who strayed from those principles very often found themselves in serious trouble. Today, in the police college and on the job, the principles of Sir Robert Peel are taught to all recruits.

In my early years the police were the responsibility of the governor and the colonial government. In 1964 there were constitutional revisions, but the police and internal security remained under the control of the colonial government. In 1968 the police and internal security became the responsibility of a cabinet minister for the first time, with the governor retaining ultimate control. A police service commission was appointed by the governor, reportedly to lessen the likelihood of political meddling and to play a monitoring role. In 1966, when Queen Elizabeth and Prince Phillip visited The Bahamas, we were officially renamed the Royal Bahamas Police Force. The 1960s were a period of reform, as the force grew in numbers and responsibilities. With new divisions, sections and units the force became more efficient and effective.

Political Independence from Britain came on July 10 1973, although The Bahamas remained a member of the Commonwealth of Nations. For the first time, Bahamians took full control of the police, although our allegiance to the queen (through her local representative, the governor-general, remained intact. Those of us in the police service, who had the good fortune to attend training courses and seminars in the United Kingdom, knew that the system of policing is nothing but reflection of the community and its concepts of justice. When society undergoes change the police system adapts itself to the needs of the time. On independence, the foreign executives of our police service left a system in place that was modelled on the British system, for which most of the senior Bahamian officers had been trained and were properly prepared to administrate.

There were big changes at the top and some changes in the middle levels of command. The British officers who had served the country well for decades were removed gradually, and the process of fully Bahamianising the police service began.

When majority rule was achieved in 1967 it paved the way for the ordinary Bahamian, who had previously been excluded, to come into the mainstream of society. The changes included massive improvements to public education and social welfare, greater equality of opportunity in employment, and a significant rise in public expectations for a better life in general. All these heady developments made Bahamians happy and optimistic. At the Scottish Police College in Edinburgh I wrote a paper that boasted about the quiet and non-violent revolution taking place in The Bahamas. The African and Asian students, all senior police personnel, were both intrigued and jealous. Many were from countries where the coup d'etat (a sudden and usually violent take over of government) was the norm.

Unfortunately, in the years following independence it appeared to many of us that the top echelon of the police force was being politicised. This perception began to affect discipline in the lower ranks and the commitment of the police to the public good suffered as a result. As corruption increased during the drug years of the late 1970s and early 1980s crime began to escalate. Those who were too lazy or illiterate to take advantage of the new economic developments and opportunities took the easy road to the high life. The drug trade began exposing Bahamians to a new culture of expensive jewellery, designer clothing, and easy money. The escalation in crime did not go unnoticed because our political leaders received daily, monthly and yearly reports from the police, which contained recommendations on ways to address the rising crime wave. Most of these recommendations were ignored or their implementation delayed.

From the 1970s onwards, the credibility of the police force took a nose-dive and we often found it difficult to cope. Much of the problem was caused by a lowering of standards for recruitment. We had difficulty finding recruits who met the required standard of education, or even the physical standards. And it was well known that politicians were sending supporters to be recruited who did not meet the minimum standards. This quantitative increase without any regard for quality did not do any good for policing or for society as a whole.

During the 40 years since independence, the erosion of discipline in the police force has been a gradual, but continuous, process. The old British Army traditions went out of style, while political interference became more common. For example, the Police Staff Association succeeded in getting permission from a senior politician to march with the unions in the Labour Day parade after being denied permission by the commissioner. Police officers often failed to attend court, which led to the dismissal of criminal cases, and officers could often be seen improperly attired. There were increasing cases of negligence, often resulting in the escape of suspects in custody, and numerous examples of the police failing to provide timely assistance to victims of crime for various reasons. Many little things like the language used when answering telephone calls or addressing higher ranking officers also fell by the wayside. I know that recruits leaving the Police College were well-trained, well-groomed and mannerly. The problem appeared to lie at the supervisory level in the divisions and stations. Recruits began to discern the slackness and become slack themselves.

When Gerald Bartlett took over as commissioner in 1981 there were many critics who condemned the Bahamian police as corrupt, brutal and lacking esprit de corps. Bartlett immediately took on the task of changing public opinion and restoring morale and credibility. He regularly communicated his determination to restore excellence in the force, especially in the prevention and detection of crime. He set out to improve living and working conditions for officers, and to upgrade training and re-training programmes. Overseas training opportunities were re-instituted, and commanders were given their due in formulating policies and decision-making.

I was not on the force for long once Bartlett assumed command, but I continued to stay in touch with him after my retirement. The international publicity over drug trafficking through The Bahamas helped in his efforts to restore the integrity efficiency, and effectiveness of the police.

Those efforts were continued by Paul Farquharson, who succeeded Bartlett as commissioner, and who did a

Paul Farquharson

remarkable job with his introduction of community policing. As a result of these efforts, the present image of the police has been enhanced in the minds of the public. Despite an often unfair press and a soaring crime trend, the men and women of the Royal Bahamas Police Force continue to work diligently, displaying the courage needed to uphold the proud traditions of their predecessors.

CHAPTER 15

Corruption and the Drug Wars

The dictionary defines 'corrupt' as "ready to act immorally or illegally, especially for money." From a law enforcement perspective the most acceptable definition would be "the abuse or illegal use of office for direct or indirect pecuniary gain of the individual official, e.g; politician, policeman, customs officer, judges, magistrates, building inspectors and prosecutors."

This definition covers a range of clearly corrupt conduct, such as shaking down traffic violators for money, allowing contraband into the country, failing to investigate and prosecute criminal activity, failing to deport criminals from the country, interfering with police operations, and condoning criminal misconduct, to name just a few.

There are many ways to make money illegally. The labourer who steals from his employer, the customs officer who abets smuggling, the judge whose decision is influenced by money or pressure, and the policeman whose behaviour is modified by bribery. There are high and low risk occupations in terms of corruption, but no occupational group has a monopoly on moral, ethical and righteous behaviour - not even the clergy.

In The Bahamas and internationally, there are codes of ethical conduct that apply to politicians, law enforcement officers, judges and clergymen. These are important, provided they are an operational reality and can be enforced impartially. And the man in the street must be aware that a code of ethics is being enforced in order for it to set an example for his own conduct.

Very often codes of conduct are just documents on shelves or decorations on walls, often ignored by those in authority. Policemen detest being singled out by the public when corruption is being discussed. Corruption in policing is merely a slice of the larger problem of official corruption. This point could not be made more clearly than it was during the drug years in The Bahamas. And official corruption must be of special concern in any democratic society.

In the late 1970s and early 1980s the Bahamas was engaged in a war with foreign criminal organisations dedicated to transporting huge amounts of illicit drugs from

South America to North America. Carlos Lehder was the transport chief of the Medellin cartel and he set up a company called International Dutch Resources, which became the owner of Norman's Cay in the Exumas. At one point American officials - referring to the frequency of drug flights - said the little island's airstrip was as busy as Chicago's O'Hare International Airport.

Eventually, the breadth and depth of the trafficker's use of the Bahamas was unveiled in a dramatic NBC television news report broadcast on September 5 1983. It contained allegations about massive corruption in The Bahamas, but these reports were nothing new to many of us in the police. In fact, even before the drug wars began we observed a disturbing trend in which cases against influential people were not being prosecuted.

I was involved in two investigations of members of parliament, both of which were prima facie cases. In other words, there was convincing evidence of the involvement of these politicians in the theft of public funds. One was chairman of the National Insurance Board. He was found to be depositing money from NIB via cheque to his personal account. A permanent secretary had been asked to co-sign the cheques, but refused to do so. Our evidence was airtight, as proven during the preliminary inquiry in the Magistrate's Court, but the case was never brought to the Supreme Court for trial.

The other MP was chairman of the Broadcasting Corporation. Auditors determined that he had been using his official credit card for personal expenses - to the tune of many thousands of dollars. A senior manager at the corporation made sure that the credit card invoices were promptly paid with BCB funds. The chairman also wrote cheques payable to himself, which were co-signed by the same manager and very often cashed by a messenger. We had proof of the chairman using corporate cash to pay for air travel for his friends and relatives, women's clothing, hotel rooms and even gambling debts. The MP was arrested and I recall his wife saying to me that her husband would never be prosecuted. She was right. The case did not even reach the preliminary inquiry stage.

We could never understand why these matters were not prosecuted. But what was most disturbing to me as the investigator was not only the amount of effort involved and the man hours spent on the case, but the fact that two veteran civil servants were unfairly dismissed without a pension. Both unfortunately died just a few years later.

During the same period, Loftus Roker, who was then minister of health, reported that massive thefts were taking place at the Princess Margaret Hospital. The report was made to Commissioner Salathiel Thompson, who assigned me to conduct the investigation. We discovered that a senior hospital employee who could approve purchase orders was abusing his authority. Thousands of dollars worth of goods ordered from Taylor Industries at the hospital's expense had been delivered to private homes. We executed search warrants to recover these items and the consignees made statements confirming that they were gifts from the hospital employee. But at the end of the investigation Roker was transferred to another ministry. When I advised the commissioner of my intention to arrest the hospital official he sent the file be sent to the attorney-general's office, as is usually the case in such matters. After several weeks Thompson told me that prosecution of the official had been waived and the stolen items were to be consigned to the hospital.

But these experiences were just the smoke as the fire began to ignite. The blaze was yet to come. As the 1970s progressed many of my colleagues became distressed at what we saw taking place around us. Men like Courtney Strachan of Special Branch, Lawrence Major of the Marine Division, and Dudley Hanna of the Family Islands Division could see a trend developing - policemen were often volunteering for duty on the out islands and it was apparent that their lifestyles were improving as a result.

Dudley Hanna

As time passed, many of us became concerned about corruption in the higher echelon of the public service, and there were reasons to suspect that it had even reached the executive level. Our efforts to co-operate with international enforcement agencies to prevent a take-over of our islands by the drug cartels were often resisted by higher authorities. Lawrence Major and the Marine Division in particular were engaged in a major struggle and were very successful in capturing traffickers and seizing large caches of drugs that were being landed throughout the archipelago. But this operational effectiveness was not to last.

Airstrips were necessary for the refuelling of the drug planes and there were dozens of them on isolated islands and cays throughout The Bahamas. The traffickers had local agents on the islands who provided lights on the airstrips for night landings, usually with vehicles strategically parked. They would supply fuel from tanks hidden in the bushes. Officials from the US Drug Enforcement Administration met with me to discuss blowing deep craters into these isolated runways. The DEA would provide the helicopter, the experts and the explosives while we would provide police escorts. The airstrips were identified by police intelligence and none were for use by commercial flights.

A memo was sent to the commissioner outlining our plan to destroy the landing strips, but we did not get the approval. I was told privately that the government wanted commercial aircraft to be able to use the airstrips in emergencies, but we knew they were only good for small planes and were uncharted anyway. So the airstrips remained operational and the drugs continued to flow through our Islands.

Even more telling were the instructions we received that any anti-drug operations involving overseas agencies had to be approved by the attorney-general. It appeared that our successful joint operations with the DEA were not well regarded by the political authorities and did not receive the full support of the government. There were always stumbling blocks in our way. Traffickers would know the flight plans of police aircraft, especially when Major or any of his officers were on board. Major's disclosure to the 1984 Commission of Inquiry was one of several such instances when smugglers benefitted from the poor decisions made by government officials.

We had reports from Special Branch on foreigners involved in drug trafficking in The Bahamas who could easily have been deported. But they were allowed to remain in the country. Carlos Lehder was chief among them, but there were many others who were able to continue their criminal activities unabated.

The opportunities to collect large bribes from drug traffickers resulted in widespread corruption. A young sergeant named Kenneth Clarke worked in my office at District Headquarters while studying for his "A" levels. When the police officer stationed in San Salvador applied for vacation leave Clarke agreed to replace him, thinking that he would have more time for his studies. Once on the island Clark was approached by two Columbian-Americans who advised him to ignore the arrival of their aircraft for refuelling on its way to the US. They gave him $10,000 in cash plus a Rolex watch for the favour. Clarke appeared to accept the bribe and then contacted me. I arranged for the police aircraft to collect him on their patrol and bring him to Nassau, where he showed me the watch and the money. We immediately met with the commissioner and an armed police task force was sent to arrest the Colombians as they refuelled their aircraft loaded with cocaine at San Salvador.

Police on the Family Islands had to be very careful when making such reports by telephone. The drug culture had spread through the islands like wildfire and no-one could be sure who was listening in on phone conversations. The raid that I led on Bimini had put a dent in the trafficking operations in that area for a short period. But it was successful only because the details of the plan were restricted to a handful of senior officers and the men who typed the search warrants, which were signed by Magistrate Wilton Hercules. The men who took part in the raid were completely in the dark until we neared Bimini in the Defence Force ships that we boarded in Freeport. Secrecy was key, and we never understood why the same procedure was not used for the higher-profile raid on Norman's Cay, which failed miserably. The assumption was that the failure was due to the corruption of senior personnel. I know that American law enforcement agencies were dumbfounded that there were no seizures or arrests during that raid.

I was visited once by an American lawyer at District Headquarters in Nassau. As soon as he walked in the door I knew he was involved with organized crime in some way. The dark suit, silk shirt, gold watch, alligator skin shoes and shiny leather briefcase were clear trademarks. He said he had been referred to me by a local attorney who was also a member of parliament. He wanted bail for two men held at Exuma on drug charges. They had been arrested by Lawrence Major with a plane on which 200 kilos of cocaine was found. I told him our policy was not to grant bail to foreigners arrested with large amounts of drugs, but he could always appeal to the commissioner. At this point he opened his briefcase, which was full of packets of hundred dollar bills. I quickly sent him packing.

In those years, my contacts at the DEA and FBI told many stories about the cruelty of drug dealers - so much so that I developed an intense fear and dislike for those men, especially the foreigners. A number of police officers were very worried about the pervasive corruption in the country, and about what we were likely to encounter during raids and investigations if security had been compromised. In the year before the NBC broadcast many policemen realized that the country was actively condoning drug trafficking. High-level elected officials and civil servants were providing aid and comfort for the drug barons, and the integrity of our police force was under massive threat due to our inability to function in certain areas without what appeared to be directions from higher authority. There was so much more we could have done at the time to counter the threat, but were sadly not at liberty to do.

For instance, we knew of a place on Bay Street where foreign "investors" frequently met with local politicians and their gofers. The news media often referred to that place in their articles and the FBI were interested in many of the persons who went there. These people could easily have been apprehended and deported.

The dramatic NBC revelations in 1983 had the salutary effect of forcing the Bahamian people to take stock of what was happening in their own country. The infamous Miami Herald headline - A Nation for Sale - caused a lot of embarrassment for Bahamians, especially when travelling overseas. And the 1984 Commission of Inquiry in Nassau confirmed a lot of our suspicions as policemen. I recall Magistrate Max Thompson lamenting the 'lost generation' of Bahamians whose lives had been destroyed by drugs. The drug years also spawned Bahamian criminal gangs who carried on the nefarious trade after the Colombian operations had been shut down.

That period of widespread corruption and illegal trafficking changed the whole culture of The Bahamas - for good and for bad. Some of the biggest drug dealers of that era are now in prison, either here or in the United States. And the shame and scandal emanating from the Commission of Inquiry caused many high ranking officials to repent their ways. The illegal drug trade still exists today, but thankfully the police are not being obstructed in their work.

Those officers who succumbed to corruption during those terrible years may well have been influenced by what they knew to be happening among the leading citizens of the nation. For example, a religious leader at the time became infamous for his statement that "principle don't put bread on the table."

Prime Minister Lynden Pindling on camera being interview by Brian Ross on NBC-TV in 1983. Pindling accused Ross of being a "faker".

CHAPTER 16

International Police Relations– from Angela Davis to *HMBS Flamingo*

As a boy growing up in Trinidad, my grandfather, Granville Pilgrim, often spoke of his police service in British Guiana (now Guyana) and told mar.y stories of his encounters with dastardly criminals. He had great respect for the US Federal Bureau of Investigation and Britain's Scotland Yard, calling them the world's best crime-fighting agencies.

At Cunupia Village we had no television or radio in the 1930s and 40s. Our entertainment was to read books and newspapers. And I would often read about the legendary exploits of J. Edgar Hoover of the FBI. I never met Hoover, but in effect he became my mentor. My first meeting with a real FBI agent happened many years later when I investigated a case of land fraud in Nassau.

During the trial, Magistrate Maxwell Thompson ordered the police to find and interrogate a person of interest to the defence who lived in Florida. Arrangements were made with the FBI and I was sent on my first visit to the United States. An African-American agent named Leo MacLaren met me at the Miami Airport, and to my great delight he was a close associate of FBI Director Hoover. In fact, he was responsible for Hoover's safety whenever he visited Miami (where he often went on vacation). MacLaren and his wife Lossie accommodated me in their home, and I was able to learn a lot about the agency. I never met Hoover, but I knew that under his leadership, the FBI had became an integral part of American government and an icon of popular culture.

FBI labs provided advanced forensic services to other law enforcement agencies, and The Bahamas would soon benefit from these services as our relationship with the Americans developed. Many personal relationships were forged between FBI agents in the Miami office and detectives in the Royal Bahamas Police Force, an exchange that benefitted both organizations. Although I never met Hoover, I was able to meet other FBI directors who visited The Bahamas over the years, including Clarence Kelley, William

Webster and Louis Freeh.

The principles governing international criminal police cooperation and its working methods evolved gradually over the years, and I think it is true to say that the Royal Bahamas Police Force, and in particular the Criminal Investigation Department, led the way in developing ties with other law enforcement agencies in the Caribbean, in North and South America and in Europe.

Professional relationships and friendships were developed when Bahamian police officers attended training courses and seminars at home or abroad. These relationships meant that we could get information or help when we needed

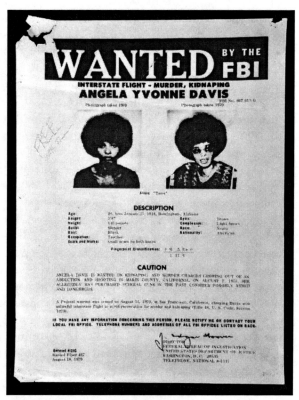

Angela Davis' FBI wanted poster.

it most. There were no letters or red tape involved, unless it absolutely could not be avoided. It was simply a matter of one agency communicating its needs to another.

In the 1950s and 60s a lot of our lab work was done in Jamaica, through our co-operation with the Jamaica Constabulary. They had a lab - we didn't. So they provided assistance with drug testing, blood work, firearms examination and handwriting analysis. I had the privilege of visiting Jamaica frequently to take exhibits in criminal trials for analysis at the laboratory, which at the time was headed by a forensic pathologist named Ellington. He testified as the firearms examiner in the murder case against Talbot "Stokes" Thompson in the 1950s. We also exchanged information on outstanding arrest warrants. And this included checking Bahamian Immigration Department files for the names of persons wanted by the Jamaica Constabulary, for example.

In later years similar co-operation was developed with US enforcement agencies, including the Federal Bureau of Investigation, the Drug Enforcement Administration, the Secret Service and US Customs and Immigration. FBI agents visited the Bahamas on a monthly basis and many close friendships were developed with Bahamian officers, which resulted in expeditious assistance on criminal matters. In addition, many Bahamian officers attended training courses in the US, or US-administered courses held in The Bahamas. As drug trafficking expanded in the mid 1970s, DEA agents were always in the islands and many personal relationships were developed. It was during this period that we moved our drug testing and lab work from Jamaica to Florida, which worked out to be less costly. It also turned out that our requests were handled more expeditiously.

All of these relationships were maintained without governmental or political involvement and, in fact, many were kept confidential for years - in some cases, not even senior police officers knew of them. The chief benefit was being able to avoid paperwork, which often led to leaks of vital information. I know that my own relationships with US FBI, DEA and Secret Service agents led to many arrests in The Bahamas and abroad - some of which are recorded in this book.

Bahamian police provided assistance to the Americans in many areas, including surveillance of US citizens in The Bahamas. We monitored organised crime chief Santos Trafficante while he was living in an upscale Freeport apartment during the 1960s. We also monitored the African-American activist Angela Davis, who was under surveillance by the FBI for her involvement with the Communist Party of the USA and the Black Power movement. She spent a weekend in Freeport under the watchful eyes of Detective Inspector Ormond Briggs, Detective Sergeant Arthur Yearwood and myself. I had the opportunity to speak with her in a hotel bar in Freeport. I introduced myself as a school-teacher from Trinidad and we had a delightful conversation. She was highly intelligent and well educated, and I felt badly about the deception, but it was all a part of police work. Davis was later placed on the FBI's Most Wanted list and was arrested in 1970 on charges of conspiracy, kidnapping and homicide. It was alleged that she participated in a courtyard escape attempt by George Jackson of the Black Panther Party, in which the judge was shot to death. She was detained for about two years in a women's detention centre In New York City before being exonerated of all charges.

In 1975 we received information from the FBI that a Top Ten fugitive named Thomas Edward Bethea was in Nassau. He was seen gambling in the Paradise Island casino, betting $50 on each roll of the dice. FBI agents from Miami were allowed into the country with their weapons, while I arranged for four detectives to apprehend Bethea and bring him to CID. We arrested a black man at the craps table who fitted Bethea's general descrip-tion, but a fingerprint check with the FBI confirmed that we had the wrong man in custody. Eventually, we got the right man. Bethea was wanted for kidnapping and it was believed that he had deposited his ransom money at a Nassau bank. I obtained a search warrant and visited the bank with John Rolle and an FBI agent who identified the money by the serial numbers. Bet-  hea was quickly deported on a flight to Miami, where he was arrested. Bethea was a professional boxer in the light heavyweight division.

John Rolle

A drug raid on the island of Bimini was very successful due to the fact that under-cover agents sent there in advance provided excellent intelligence, which was communi-cated to Commissioner Salathial Thompson. I was ordered to conduct the raid, and the only others who knew of the operation were Dudley Hanna, who was then in charge of the Grand Bahama Division; Arthur Yearwood, a CID officer who prepared the search warrants; and Magistrate Wilton Hercules, who authorised the warrants and allowed us to retain the court copies until the operation was over.

Officers from the CID and uniformed branches were selected and equipped for travel, but not told anything about the destination. We left on a charter flight for Freeport, where we boarded two Defence Force vessels late that night.

On the way to Bimini we held a briefing and all personnel were given their assignments. A former policeman from Bimini named Ivan Wallace accompanied the raiding party to identify the houses to be searched. The operation was a great success - several arrests were made and large quantities of cocaine and marijuana were seized.

The team was commended by the Commissioner and all of those arrested pleaded guilty and were fined large sums of money. These fines were paid by the drug baron of Bimini. When he died a few years later, his funeral was attended by several cabinet ministers.

On another occasion we received information that the vice president of a company on Paradise Island was seeking a buyer for five kilos of cocaine. My informant advised that a search of the residence, which was a hotel room, would prove fruitless. I kept this information to myself, but contacted Fred Dick, the DEA chief in Florida, to develop a plan for undercover agents to meet the suspect. Through surveillance I learned that the suspect frequented a particular bar where he would socialise with beautiful women. The DEA chief sent a rasta-looking male agent and a very attractive female agent to participate in the sting. Their job was to hang out at the bar, strike up a friendship with the suspect, and eventually seek to buy the cocaine.

A week after their arrival they were able to negotiate a deal, but the suspect wanted to see cash. I arranged with a local bank manager to place a large amount of cash in a safe deposit box for the suspect to view. The undercover agents gave the suspect the key to the box and the suspect agreed to deliver the cocaine to the agents in their room at the Holiday Inn. CID officers entered from an adjoining room and made the arrest. This operation was also successful because I kept tight control on information, only sharing it with those in a need to know. Commissioner Thompson commended me for the sting and the suspect - who was an American citizen - was subsequently jailed.

A third incident involved information about a large load of marijuana stored on a boat at Eleuthera that had recently arrived from Jamaica. There were five local men on board seeking a buyer for the ganja. We learned that a police sergeant in Nassau was the contact for the sale, and I discussed this with Fred Dick of the Florida DEA. Undercover agents again visited Nassau and made contact with the sergeant, who put them in touch with the vendors on Eleuthera. The DEA provided a large yacht for this sting and the marijuana was transferred off the coast at Hatchet Bay. Police photographers were able to record the transaction from shore.

Payment in US dollars was to be made to the sergeant in a room at the British Colonial Hotel in Nassau after the drugs had been transferred. Again, police entered from an adjoining room and arrested the sergeant as he was collecting the cash. Officers at Eleuthera arrested the five men who had sold the drugs. We kept this operation secret from politicians and senior officials.

At another time, we received information that a large number of stolen vehicles from the US were being sold in Freeport. I was then in charge of the CID unit on Grand Bahama, so I met with the head of Customs in Freeport and asked for documentation on all vehicles that had arrived on the island over the past six months, as well as weekly reports on new imports. All of this was communicated to the FBI in Miami who soon began sending us notifications of stolen vehicles. Subsequent investigations led to the arrest of five Americans living in high style at the posh neighbourhood known as Bahamia. They were deported to the US and prosecuted as part of a large vehicle smuggling ring operating in South Florida. Individuals in Freeport who had purchased the stolen vehicles were allowed to keep them in return for testifying against the thieves in court.

In most of the matters needing international coordination an FBI agent named Gerard Forrester was involved. In fact, Forrester visited Nassau so often that he became one of us, and was able to develop many information sources locally. He was a legend at CID.

In 1980 I was directly involved in the gravest international incident ever to take place on Bahamian territory, which led to significant collaboration with the Americans. This incident was the sinking of the Royal Bahamas Defence Force patrol boat, *HMBS Flamingo*, in 1980.

HMBS Flamingo in better days.

The Flamingo's crew had intercepted and arrested two Cuban fishing vessels found poaching near Ragged Island. As the *Flamingo* headed for Duncan Town with the fishing boats in tow, Cuban warplanes suddenly appeared and began strafing the patrol boat. After the vessel had been sunk and four marines killed, the Cuban fighters flew off and the *Flamingo's* survivors commandeered one of the fishing boats and arrived in Duncan Town with eight Cuban poachers some five hours later, when they were able to radio Nassau for help.

I accompanied Police Commissioner Salathial Thompson and Defence Force Commodore William Swinley (a former British naval officer) to Duncan Town on a chartered Bahamasair DC-3. We arrived to an astonishing sight - there were Cuban troops on the ground at the airport, and Cuban helicopters and jet fighters were buzzing the settlement. We quickly retired to a building where the surviving crewmen and poachers were located and began questioning them. I was instructed to relay the information we received back to Nassau, where the cabinet was waiting anxiously for news.

By this time, the warplanes were buzzing the little house where the entire Bahamian high command was based. As I stepped outside and headed for the telecoms office, I saw a gunner in one of the helicopters point his machine gun at me, so I quickly put my hands in the air while walking slowly towards BaTelCo. When I was finally able to reach Deputy Commissioner Gerald Bartlett in Nassau I told him we were in a virtual war zone. In fact, we fully expected Cuban troops to move out from the airport and retrieve the fishermen in our custody. But after about an hour or so the warplanes suddenly disappeared.

I went into the street and saw people pointing towards the sky - the US Air Force had arrived! We rushed to the airport with the *Flamingo* survivors and the Cuban fishermen, boarded the Bahamasair plane, and returned to Nassau, escorted by American jets. "God Bless America", I remarked to the others. Later, the Miami Herald reported that two US Marine Corps Phantom jets had been dispatched to the Ragged Island area after a US Coast Guard helicopter had been harassed by Cuban warplanes while searching for survivors of the doomed *HMBS Flamingo*.

The next three weeks saw round after round of diplomatic exchanges with the Cubans, whose vice minister of foreign affairs flew to Nassau twice to meet with External Affairs Minister Paul Adderley. When the Bahamas threatened to take the case to the United Nations, the Cubans took full responsibility for the attack, and paid compensation to the families of the dead marines. The eight Cuban poachers who started it all eventually paid $90,000 in fines.

CHAPTER 17

The Winsinger Killing

The emphasis we placed on examination and interviews at the scene of the crime was an important factor in this murder investigation. Stanley Moir was an expert in scenes of crime investigation and it was my good fortune to watch this master at work on many occasions.

The idea is to record the details of the crime scene in writing and in photographs. In a murder investigation, this would include the state and position of the body, and the location of any items that could be connected to the crime. Photography was very important to this process and we relied heavily on MacDonald Chase, who was our photography and fingerprint expert, to make deductions from the crime scene records. Interviewing people who were on the scene are also important to any investigation. Information from witnesses could guide us in the right direction.

Prior to 1900 forensic evidence was given by police officers and doctors, who had to take a lot of time to be well-prepared. But new technologies and methodologies have enabled police forces to be much more effective. The police are ready and equipped to use science in the fight against crime. For example, the discovery of DNA fingerprinting in the 1980s placed an awesome weapon at the disposal of crime investigators.

It was about 4.30 am on the 5th August 1965 when we received a report of a death at a commune at the junction of Gladstone and Carmichael Roads. It was first considered a traffic accident, but later reported as a violent homicide. Inspector Anthony Fields and I arrived at the scene at 5 am and were later joined by Inspector MacDonald Chase and a number of recently recruited female police officers, who were being trained at CID. The women included Dorothy Davis, Esther Stubbs and Norma Clarke.

Fields and Chase examined the scene while Chase recorded the details on film. I interviewed Rev Rudolph Karl Winsinger. The Winsingers - Rudolph Karl and his wife Esther Mildred - were missionaries who lived in a two-storey building on Carmichael Road owned by Island Missionary Society of The Bahamas. Winsinger told me his wife had left their bedroom during the night to get some water when he heard her screaming downstairs. Rushing to her aid, he collided with her at the top of the stairs and she toppled to the bottom where he found that she was dead. I asked him about the bed linen I saw under her body at the bottom of the stairs and he said he had used it to comfort her as she lay dying at the foot of the stairs.

I noticed that there were blood stains on different sides of the staircase, that I suspected were made by someone going up and down the steps. It also appeared that the bloodstains on one side of the steps were heavier than on the other. In my tour of the building I found no female clothing or shoes in the bedroom closet. Packed suitcases lay on the floor of the closet and it was obvious to me that Esther Mildred Winsinger had been planning to go on a trip. I asked Rev Winsinger about the packed clothing and he said his wife was about to take a vacation. But I thought it strange for someone going on vacation to pack all of their clothing and shoes.

In the bedroom I noticed what appeared to be spots of blood on the ceiling. I also learned that the Winsinger's had a son, who on the night of the murder was sleeping out with friends. Fields and I suspected that Mrs. Winsinger had been attacked in the bedroom and that a fall from the top of the stairs could not have caused the injury we saw to her head, so we decided to take Rev. Winsinger to CID for further interrogation.

While at the scene Dr. Peter John Bennetts visited and pronounced Mrs. Winsinger dead. I showed Dr Bennetts the bloodstains on the steps and he agreed that they appeared to be heavier on one side. The shape and the pattern of the heavy stains indicated to him that they were made coming down the steps while the lighter stains were made going up.

It also appeared to me that someone had attempted to clean up the bedroom, but did not do a proper job. The remnants of bloodstains were still visible and I was able to remove what appeared to be dried blood from the bathroom face basin, which indicated that someone had washed their bloodstained hands in the sink. We began a thorough search inside and outside of the building for a possible weapon, which was likely to be a heavy blunt instrument.

We found bloodstains on the stairs, on the ceiling of the bedroom, in the bathroom, on the bedroom floor and hidden under a portion of the bedstead at the head of the bed. Outside, in a garbage bin, one of the policewomen found a heavy brass reading lamp with a thick base to which some hairs and hardened blood and bone fragments were attached. It was obvious that something violent had taken place in the Winsinger's bedroom.

At CID I first interviewed Winsinger's teenage son, who offered no information except that he was leaving on a vacation with his mother. Before speaking to Rev. Winsinger I was able to read the preliminary report of Dr. Joan Read, the hospital pathologist who had conducted an autopsy. Death had been caused by a heavy blow to the head with a blunt instrument. A fall down the steps was ruled out. Photos of the body showed a gaping wound that opened the head, and there were photos of all the bloodstains we had found around the house. The lamp had been identified as one that was usually on a bedside table in the Winsinger's suite. The bloodstains were removed for laboratory examination. At CID, Fields and I discussed the circumstances of the case and the available evidence before talking to Winsinger, who by this time was regarded as a suspect.

In his CID interview, Winsinger stuck to his initial statement that his wife had died falling down the stairs, but I told him that all the evidence indicated that she had been attacked and killed in the bedroom. We showed him the photographs and the blood-stained reading lamp but he did not respond to any of our suggestions or questions. Finally he said: "I love my wife and don't remember doing anything like this." It seemed he was about to confess.

Fields then took out a large photograph of his wife laid out on the table in the mortuary showing the gaping wound in her head. At this point Winsinger broke down and began sobbing. He said his wife was leaving after accusing him of having an affair with Mary Godet, the wife of a fellow pastor who lived in the same commune. I put it to him, (based on information we had received) that he and a woman were seen the night of the murder in a car outside a chicken shack on Wulff Road. He told us he had given Mrs Godet a lift and they had stopped to get a meal. He admitted spending a lot of time with Mrs Godet that night, but it was due to the fact that her husband was away. He told us that when he got home his wife started nagging him about the relationship she accused him of having with Mrs. Godet.

At some point he lost his temper and hit her with the reading lamp, which was on the bedside table. There was a lot of blood. He lifted her in the bedspread and took her out to make it look as if she had fallen down the steps, before cleaning up the bedroom as best he could. By this time Winsinger was very remorseful and began praying, but he continued to deny any relationship with Mrs Godet. We recorded his statement, which he read over and signed.

After Rev Winsinger was charged with the murder of his wife, we interviewed Mrs Godet, who also denied having an affair with Rev. Winsinger. She said she had heard screams coming from the Winsinger residence at about 2.30 am. She saw the reverend who told her there had been a terrible accident. Winsinger then went to a neighbour's house to report the accident.

During the months following Rev. Winsinger 's arraignment I was verbally harassed by his associates, who could not believe he had killed his wife. Some of these people dressed like nuns and whenever they saw me they would stop and say they were praying for me because I had framed "that poor man." I also received telephone calls from people making the same accusations. Inspector Fields was also targeted, but to a lesser extent.

In October 1965 Rev Rudolph Karl Winsinger appeared in the Supreme Court for his trial. The prosecutors were Gerald Collett, acting attorney-general, and J. Henry Bostwick, acting crown counsel. The defence attorneys were Eugene Dupuch, Leomard Knowles and Jeannie Thompson. Jury selection was a long process. Of the 25 jurors called , 13 were challenged. Eventually Harcourt Maura was elected foreman of the all-male jury.

In his opening address to the jury Collet said the evidence showed that Winsinger had killed his wife intentionally by repeatedly bashing her on the head with the lamp following an argument about an illicit affair. The prosecution's case was supported by the circumstantial evidence, the bloodstains, and Winsinger's own confession. Dupuch accused the police of pressuring him to sign the confession, but it was admitted into evidence.

Testifiying on his own behalf, Rev Winsinger told the court that he had been in custody from 5 am until he was charged at 11 pm. He said I never told him he was free to leave if he wanted to, that he was not offered breakfast, lunch or supper, and prevented from leaving CID when friends came to take him to lunch. He said Fields had advised him to tell the story about a fight with his wife and the judge might go easy on him. Winsinger also gave evidence of memory loss and other medical problems.

Collett's address to the jury was brief. He reminded them of the blood in the bedroom, the blood, bone fragments and hair on the reading lamp, and the evidence of Dr. Joan Read of multiple cuts to the head and a fracture of the skull caused by a heavy blunt instrument.

Dupuch's address to the jury took 70 minutes. He asserted that the accused did not kill his wife, but if he did he was suffering from epilepsy or some other condition that caused temporary memory loss. He reminded the jury of Winsinger's evidence of plane crashes, and the testimony of local and foreign medical experts, including Dr. Henry Podlewski, as well as several character witnesses (including Dupuch's brother, Etienne, publisher of *The Tribune*).

But on October 27, 1965 Rev Rudolph Karl Winsinger, former sergeant in the United States Air Force and missionary to The Bahamas, was found guilty of manslaughter. He was sentenced to 12 years and transferred to an American prison to serve his term.

CHAPTER 18

A Case of Piracy—and Murder

The Bahama Islands were once known as the republic of pirates. In the early 18th century fierce rebels like Edward Teach (also known as Blackbeard) were the scourge of marine commerce until the British appointed a royal governor named Woodes Rogers, who led a military crack-down that restored order to the sea lanes passing through and around The Bahamas.

In more recent years, cruising through these islands became a major tourist attraction for those with the time and money to enjoy it. And one of the most scenic cruising grounds in the Bahamian archipelago is the Exuma Cays, which stretch 130 miles from the southeastern tip of New Providence to the island of Great Exuma - where the main district settlement of Georgetown is located. In between there are numerous small cays, and atolls, but only a handful of isolated communities.

This stunningly beautiful chain of islands was the setting for one of the most dramatic examples of modern-day piracy that I can remember. In 1960, police received information that a group of people had been abandoned on an uninhabited cay in the Exumas. The information came from the pilot of a small aircraft, who observed what he described as a signal for help on the cay.

In the days before the formation of the Royal Bahamas Defence Force there was a Police Marine Division, which was headed by Lawrence Major. He proceeded to the cay and found 15 men and women who had been without food and water for several days. They were all brought to Nassau and given medical treatment.

These people were affluent, middle-aged American tourists who had chartered a yacht in South Florida to cruise the Bahamas. While in the Exumas , the charterboat captain - Angus Boatwright -had spotted a small boat in distress and offered assistance. Two young Americans - Alvin Table and Billy Wayne Sees - were brought on board the charter yacht, after which they produced guns and took over the ship, killing Boatwright when he tried to resist. The passengers were then robbed and left on the uninhabited cay. It seemed that piracy had returned to the Bahamas.

Albert Miller headed up a team of detectives who interviewed all the survivors, while McDonald Chase lifted fingerprints from the small boat left behind by the pirates. From these prints the FBI were able to identify Table and Sees. Information on the stolen charter yacht was circulated throughout the region and several days later we got word that the pirates had been arrested in Cuba.

But this was during a time of rising tension between the United States and Cuba, where Fidel Castro was busy entrenching himself as the island's undisputed communist leader. In 1959 the CIA had put out a contract on Castro's life, and the Cubans were naturally touchy about Americans showing up uninvited. The British Embassy in Havana had to negotiate carefully with the Castro government to secure the handover of both the pirates and the stolen vessel.

I was one of the officers selected to go to Cuba and take custody of the two men. Other officers in the party were Albert Miller, Edney Johnson, Errington Watkins, Courtney Strachan and Frank Russell, the Englishman in charge of CID at the time.

We left Nassau early in the morning on a Bahamas Airways charter flight and flew straight into the most violent storm I have ever experienced. As the plane was being tossed about like a matchstick, my fellow officers were praying for their lives. And when Albert Miller started singing the tragic hymn *Nearer my God to Thee*, we all joined in.

It was not the first time I had heard Miller sing that hymn. I was with him once during a dinghy trip in Andros with a local constable when the sea became very rough and we all thought the little the boat would capsize. I remember the outboard engine cutting off several times as we were tossed about by the waves. But after a while the weather calmed and we were able to complete our journey without mishap. The same thing happened on the flight to Havana.

A British Embassy official met us at the airport and escorted us to the prison where the two Americans were being held. We were searched by soldiers with automatic weapons and then taken to a compound inside the prison. While we were waiting Watkins lit up a cigarette and was immediately surrounded by troops offering to exchange their

The Police Marine Division's first four patrol boats docked at Nassau. The Division was created in 1971 to combat illegal immigration, poaching and drug trafficking.

Cuban smokes for his American cigarettes. I found this odd considering the reputation Cuba has for growing quality tobacco.

Eventually, the two American prisoners were released to us and we left Cuba on the charter flight with the two pirates in custody.

On the journey back to Nassau the Americans were quite chatty. They told some horrendous stories about their time in the Cuban jail - especially the frequent fights that were stopped by the guards firing over the prisoners' heads and slowly moving the line of fire down until all the inmates were hugging the ground to avoid being shot.

In Nassau the two Americans were charged with piracy, kidnapping, armed robbery and murder. There was a preliminary inquiry followed by a supreme court trial, which the US Embassy followed closely. Alvin Table and Billy Wayne Sees were convicted and sentenced to death. They were hanged at Fox Hill prison on May 9, 1961.

CHAPTER 19

The Banker's Killing

Detective Sergeants Anthony Fields and Fletcher Johnson were close friends of mine and it was a privilege to work with them on many major cases over the years.

Fields was a firm, astute and articulate leader, with a keen sense of humour. He also had a photographic memory, which at times was uncanny. Johnson was an outstanding policeman and investigator, with a reputation as a ladies man, and a lot of the information he obtained during his career as a detective came from women.

I recall going to a house in Fox Hill with Fields late one night looking for a Jamaican armed robber we thought was living there. Fields went directly over to an abandoned vehicle in the yard and confronted the man we were looking for - he had been sleeping in the car and had a .38 revolver between his legs. Fields coolly warned that if the he touched the gun he would be a dead man. Fortunately, the Jamaican gave up without a fight.

On another occasion in 1965, I was taking over from the night shift at CID and was being briefed by Fields and Johnson when a call came that the Royal Bank of Canada branch on John F Kennedy Drive was being held up by a gunman. So the three of us rushed off to the scene.

Kendal Lightbourn

When we arrived at the bank we learned that the branch manager, Everette Pearce, had been killed during the robbery. Witnesses told us that the gunman had entered with a cloth covering his face and demanded money from the tellers, who quickly complied. When the manager walked into the tellers area, unaware that a robbery was taking place, the gunman shot him dead. We interviewed everyone in the bank and got a description of the gunman and his accent.

As we were leaving the bank a woman called Fletcher by his nickname, Beaver, and gave him some valuable information. As she had been about to enter the bank she had noticed that a robbery was in progress and stayed outside. When the gunman came out and removed the cloth around his face she recognised him as a taxi driver named Samuel Thompson. Although she was prepared to give this tip to Johnson, she refused to make a statement or agree to testify in court.

Johnson remained at the scene of the crime while Fields and I drove west on JFK drive - the direction that the female witness had seen the man leave in after hailing a passing taxi. At the airport we questioned all the taxi drivers we could find. One remembered seeing Thompson at the domestic terminal so we spoke to all the airline ticket agents. No scheduled flights had left for the out islands recently, but we learned that a charter flight had left for Fresh Creek Andros an hour earlier with a single male passenger, who fitted the description of the man we were looking.

Fields and I arranged for a local charter pilot to fly us to Fresh Creek. The local constable told us that Thompson had arrived on a recent charter flight and advised us where we were likely to find him over the creek. As we waited at the ferry dock the constable came by to tell us that Thompson was actually on the ferry. As soon as he stepped ashore Fields pulled out his gun and ordered Thompson to put his hands on his head, which he did.

We handcuffed Thompson and took him to a secure place for questioning. During the interview I could sense his fear. I told him we knew where he had stashed his gun and the stolen money over the creek and were in the process of getting a search warrant. At this point Thompson admitted leaving the gun and money at a relative's house. We recovered both items and returned to Nassau with our quarry.

The money was identified by marked bills and a ballistics expert from the FBI confirmed that the fatal bullet had come from Thompson's gun. The murder trial was over in a few days, and although the defence lawyer made the usual complaint that the confession had been beaten out of him, there was no evidence of any physical abuse.

It is a fact that as long as there are confessions there will be attorneys alleging that they are obtained by police brutality. But in this case, the confession was not the only evidence and Samuel Thompson was convicted and sentenced to death. He was hanged at Fox Hill prison in 1966.

Fields and I were commended for our work, but Johnson deserved a lot of the credit for being so attractive to the opposite sex.

Samuel Thompson had a brother named Ernest who was in the police force at the time. After we arrested his brother and brought him to justice, Ernest displayed a great deal of resentment towards us, so we learned to avoid him as much as we could, until he retired from the force in the 1960s.

CHAPTER 20

The Murder of Inspector Henderson Norville

In 1970, upon my return from training in police management and crime prevention at the Scottish Police College, I was transferred from the Criminal Investigation Department - where I had been posted since 1952 - to replace Gerald Bartlett as assistant commissioner in charge of the New Providence District (Uniform Branch). This post included the Family Islands, but it was purely administrative, and since I had become accustomed to the action at CID I found the new job a bit boring.

After a year I was transferred as assistant commissioner of the Grand Bahama District, replacing Bartlett again. Freeport was my favourite Bahamian town, and I had made a lot of friends there during my term as officer in charge of the Freeport CID unit from 1965 to 1968.

Although this was also an administrative position, I had more time to spend with the detectives at CID, and even managed to help with some of their investigations. Notable among those detectives were Inspectors Ormond Briggs and Kendal Lightbourn, and Sergeants Arthur Yearwood and Godfrey Knowles, all of whom had been my colleagues at CID in Nassau.

Inspector Henderson Norville, also a former detective, was posted to the Mobile Division in Freeport. He lived with his wife, a government nurse, and their children, and was one of those quiet, but effective policemen who preferred to stay out of the limelight. He was respected and loved by all of us. Norville's family was well known in Freeport as his wife endeared herself to the people she served at the clinic.

In 1974 John Crawley was assistant commissioner in charge of CID, and he told me that a man named Errol Dean, who was wanted in New Providence for several gun crimes, may have moved to Grand Bahama. Dean was armed and considered dangerous. Kendal Lightbourn, who grew up in the Bain Town/Grants Town area, knew Dean, and we had photographs of him, which we circulated to police stations. I also knew some members of the Dean family, who had befriended me during my early years in The Baha-

85

mas. But I did not know Dean himself.

After several weeks of intensive, but discreet, inquiries we received information about Dean's whereabouts. He had a girlfriend in Nassau, but had hooked up with another woman in Grand Bahama. When the Nassau woman discovered that Dean was cheating on her, we received anonymous information that Dean was living in a one-room apartment at Pinder's Point and often spent time at a local nightclub. I assumed the tip had come from Dean's jilted lover.

Investigation by Lightbourn was very discreet. We were able to identify the building and the apartment number, and learned that the proprietor of the club at Pinder's Point had rented the apartment to Dean. We also learned that Dean sometimes slept in his girlfriend's apartment in the same building. At a strategy meeting we decided against trying to capture Dean at the club so as to avoid a possible public shoot-out. Instead, we planned to offer the club owner immunity from prosecution, take him to Dean's apartment, and get him to open the door.

Seven volunteers were picked for this dangerous operation - including Kendal Lightbourn, Ormond Briggs, Godfrey Knowles and myself. At the last minute Henderson Norville asked to join the team and I agreed. Norville had been attending court in Nassau and was not expected back in Freeport until the following day. But having heard we were planning a raid, he came back early to take part. He was that kind of policeman.

We planned to pick up the club owner at 3am and take him to Dean's apartment. But at about 2am I received a strange telephone call from a former policeman in Nassau named Wilton Beach. Beach was from Tobago, where many people believe in the occult. He seemed very excited on the phone and expressed a genuine concern for my safety as he related a dream to me. He had seen me shot dead while leading a team of detectives to capture bank robbers. Beach begged me to be careful as he considered this dream to be a genuine portent of the future.

As it happened, things went terribly wrong with the operation from the start. On our first stop we discovered that the club owner had left Freeport for a few days. But we couldn't afford to abort the raid then for fear that Dean would be alerted and fly the coop.

When we arrived at his apartment, I posted two men with shotguns on the ground outside the window of the second floor unit, so that if Dean looked out he would see armed police waiting for him. The rest of us proceeded upstairs. Norville and two others went to the girlfriend's apartment where Dean sometimes stayed. Lightbourn, armed with a revolver, two sergeants with shotguns, and myself (unarmed) went to Dean's apartment. We ordered him to come out with his hands up, but to our surprise a small boy opened the door.

The boy did not respond to questions, and I heard a sound like coins or bullets falling on the floor inside the apartment. I warned Lightbourn, who was in front of me, and the two sergeants to be careful.

At this point, Norville arrived and walked directly up to the little boy. A shot rang out and he fell forward into the apartment. Lightbourn and the two sergeants both fired into the apartment. The blast from the shotguns blew a hole in the wall of the adjoining apartment, which apparently caused Dean to hit the floor. We quickly moved in and arrested him. Norville was rushed to the Rand Memorial Hospital along with Dean, who had been wounded by Lightbourn's shot. When Norville expired shortly afterwards, Ormond Briggs and I had to restrain some of the officers from attacking Dean.

The next day Freeporters were in shock mourning the death of a well-loved police officer and family man. It was one of the saddest days of my life and I had gnawing doubts as to whether my plan had caused my friend's death. For months I discussed the operation with officers at every level, and even with FBI personnel. They all assured me that there were no flaws and urged me to accept Norville's killing as an unfortunate incident. It took me a long time for this advice to sink in.

The investigation revealed that the gun recovered at the scene from Dean was a police firearm that had been issued to John Crawley - who was assistant commissioner in charge of CID at the time. Dean admitted stealing the gun from Crawley's police car while it was parked somewhere in Nassau. During Dean's murder trial, the defence attorney attempted to place responsibility for the killing on the police, but a firearms expert from the FBI confirmed that the fatal bullet had been fired from Dean's gun. Errol Dean was found guilty of the murder of Henderson Norville and was sentenced to death.

An earlier investigation had revealed that Dean was a member of a gang called the Goon Squad which tried to disrupt campaign meetings during the 1972 general election. It was assumed that this group was affiliated to the Free National Movement under the direction of party leader Cecil Wallace Whitfield, but Dean assured us that this was not the case. He said he took instructions from Dr. Curtis MacMillan, who was responsible for the formation of the squad.

He also expressed remorse over the death of Inspector Norville. It was depressing to see a young, healthy, good-looking man from a fine Bahamian family waiting to be executed, and this feeling remained with me a long time after he was hanged.

This happened at a time when violent resistance to police officers was unusual. And magistrates and judges dealt very severely with those who resisted arrest or assaulted policemen in the execution of their duty. Magistrates like Maxwell Thompson, Wilton Hercules, Emmanuel Osadebey, John Bailey and Kendal Isaacs were known to jail such criminals as a matter of course, and we appreciated the protection they provided.

Prior to the 1974 murder of Henderson Norville there was another police killing that I recall. In 1962 local constable James Adderley was patrolling with another member of the Flying Squad when they encountered a burglar in the Sears Addition neighbourhood. Adderley was fatally injured while trying to make the arrest. He was 40 years old. Following the Norville murder there were more killings of police officers - Constable Franklyn Forbes in the 1970s, Beach Warden Phillip Kelly in the 1980s, Constables Jimmy Ambrose, Stephen Butler, Truman Cooper, Raymond Rolle, Sidney Munroe, Barry Rose, Perry Munroe and Raymond Knowles in the 1990s.

In 1995 Corporals Barry Rose and Charles Ferguson were dispatched to investigate an alarm activation at a bakery on Atlantic Drive in Freeport. They encountered an armed robber, who shot Rose nine times and stabbed Ferguson with a screwdriver. The suspect, Stephen Moore was shot dead by police during another burglary attempt soon afterwards.

In the year 2000 three policemen were murdered - Constables Aaron Otis Greene and Jeffery Tucker, and Chief Inspector William Moss. These deaths were followed by the murders of Constables Terrell Smith, Ramos Williams, Desmond Burrows and Othello Robert Darville. All were killed in the line of duty. There was also the death of Inspector Archibald Miller of the Drug Enforcement Unit, who was reportedly shot while on a surveillance exercise during an illegal drug investigation, but his death was due to friendly fire.

Between 1962 and 2000 at least 17 police officers were killed in the line of duty. The Royal Bahamas Police Force, the families, and the nation grieve over these deaths at the hands of criminals. These men died serving their country and will always be remembered for that.

We are now engaged in a war, with the gun being the criminal's weapon of choice. I have always stressed the importance of police officers taking precautions to protect themselves when dealing with vicious criminals, or when about to make arrests, or even just when stopping a suspect for questioning. We would do well to remember the two policemen who were killed when they failed to search a rogue cop caught breaking into a convenience store. The average citizen doesn't realise how dangerous a routine traffic stop, warrant service, or interrogation can be.

Police officers are not trained to shoot to kill. They are trained to shoot to live. When they shoot, they are not trying to take a suspect's life. They are simply trying to survive and go home to their family. When lives are threatened, police officers have the right and the justification to use any means necessary, which includes shooting to live.

CHAPTER 21

The Police, the Press and the Lawyers

A law enforcement officer is professionally crippled if he cannot effectively communicate with the community he serves through the mass media. In The Bahamas, law enforcement and journalism are locked arm in arm by a mutual obligation to improve society and protect the dignity and security of the nation.

Significant accomplishments have resulted from active co-operation between the media and the police. Advertising the names and photos of wanted persons, and public education campaigns on crime prevention and traffic safety have been very effective. Time after time, information provided to the media has led to the early apprehension of badly wanted fugitives, or to the successful conclusion of investigations of wide public interest. The rapid dissemination by news agencies of lifesaving advice from enforcement and emergency authorities to endangered communities has many times averted loss of life and property.

As a nerve centre of national activity, law enforcement is examined and judged with every newspaper edition or radio or television newscast. Every published account that demonstrates the determination of purpose, sound judgement and professionalism of law enforcement agencies helps to confirm the futility of crime. News photographs of a police officer at work - giving sympathetic help to a person in need, firmly controlling the threat of mob action, capably executing an arrest, or disregarding personal risk to save the life of another - are eyewitness testimonies that enhance public trust.

On occasion, journalists may develop real evidence of abuse of authority in law enforcement, or gross dereliction of duty and outright corruption. Both society and law enforcement benefit by the exposure of these cancerous pockets. But the large majority of officers are well-meaning and honest - dedicated to the fair and effective administration of justice. They need to receive the encouragement and support of the press.

The key to meaningful cooperation between the police and the press is a mutual understanding of the role and procedures of each profession. Not only should enforcement executives recognise and appreciate the right of the public to be informed, they must consider it their duty to ensure that news personnel receive full and wholehearted assistance at every level of the Force. Day to day dealings with the press should promote confidence in the ability of the Force and trust in its sincerity of purpose.

In my 30 years of experience as a policeman, the Tribune in particular has always supported and publicised our efforts at solving crime in our nation. Mention must be made here of the late Lewis Bealer, who was a distinguished crime reporter for the Tribune back in the 1960s. At our request he often withheld information from publication to give us time to complete investigations.

But the relationship between law enforcement officers and attorneys is not always as cordial as the relationship with the press. It has never been so, and this is not expected to improve. The attorney's job is to prove that his client is not guilty of the crime for which he is charged. For example, where an individual is charged with possession of a firearm, they are found in physical possession of the weapon, but - when represented by an attorney - they plead not guilty. There are cases where individuals are caught inside a house or shop that was broken into. They also plead not guilty, and their attorneys request frequent adjournments, which can delay matters for months and, in a few cases that I am aware of, years. These long delays of trials are to the advantage the attorneys as they are often accompanied by the disappearance or intimidation of witnesses, the loss of case files or exhibits, and the fading memories of witnesses.

Anyone following procedures in our courts in recent times would observe the length of time it takes to complete a trial. For example, in January 2006 two men were arrested with four guns on the back seat of their car. That case was not completed until August 2011, when each received a three-year sentence. Their attorney had been able to get long adjournments. There is a case involving a woman civil servant who was arrested in 2006 for stealing a large sum of money from her department. She was charged, but the case is still pending as I write this.

Allegations of police brutality are frequently used by attorneys to defend their clients. This has been a common ploy since my days as a young recruit and it will continue to be used by attorneys in order to get written confessions thrown out by the courts. The allegations used to involve punches to the stomach, but these days we hear of beatings with baseball bats and other objects, or the use of a plastic bag to torture a suspect by preventing his breathing. But it is incorrect to say that complaints of police brutality are swept under the rug. The police investigate these claims, and some officers are awaiting trial for such misconduct. In a few instances they have been charged with causing the death of suspects held in custody. It would be fair to say that the evidence to support such allegations is often inconclusive, and in many instances flatly untrue. I know of claims of police brutality that were refuted by evidence obtained from a victim that proved the claims to be untrue.

Police officers, particularly those involved in the investigation of crime, are provided with training and administrative protocols that cover interrogation and the taking of statements. These protocols include statements of admissions to be taken under caution on a prescribed form; times of the start and completion to be recorded; words used by the suspect are not to be translated to official vocabulary; each statement page must be signed after being read over; suspects can request a copy of statement; and Judges Rules must not be contravened. Persons in custody must be told of available facilities such as toilets and their right to see a relative or an attorney, subject to certain reasonable conditions - such as the need to search for a weapon or find a child that had been kidnapped.

The Judges Rules are a guide for police investigators. They begin by saying that citizens have a duty to help a police officer to discover and apprehend offenders, and they include the admonition that any person at any stage of an investigation should be able to consult privately with an attorney. This is so even if he is in custody provided that in such case no unreasonable delay or hindrance is caused to the process of investigation or the administration of justice. Suspects must be told that they are not obliged to say anything to the police unless they wish to do so. They are also cautioned that whatever they say may be put in writing and given in evidence.

These rules were drilled into me as a young detective by Salathial Thompson and Albert Miller, who were my sergeants, and they are taught at the Police College. The rules are designed to ensure that only voluntary answers and statements are admitted in evidence against their makers, and to guide police officers in the performance of their duties. The force has its own regulations too. A full record of every arrest must be kept, including the place of custody, the times in and out for any reason, times of feeding and any visitors. There is sufficient opportunity for suspects to complain about any brutal treatment imposed by police officers.

Interrogation is a skill acquired by police officers through experience. Officers learn to evaluate a suspect's mood to discover how to obtain co-operation. Each approach is unique. I dealt with many interrogations during my career and I learned to begin by talking about the suspect's life and family before proceeding to the facts of the case. The suspect must be made to feel that police have plenty of evidence linking him to the crime. In murder cases we often produced photos of the victim, to play on their emotions or elicit feelings of remorse. An investigation must never depend solely on the contents of a confession. The goal is to find objective evidence to resolve the case.

CHAPTER 22

The Good Old Days of Policing

In the early years of my career the Royal Bahamas Police Force was a highly disciplined quasi-military organisation led by former British Army officers. The three most senior Bahamian officers - Edward Sears, Gussie Roberts and Wenzel Grainger - were also former military men. Discipline was rigidly enforced by sergeants like Stanley "Blood" Mason, Roy Armbrister, Salathial Thompson, Theophilus Gibson and Albert Miller.

Dress and appearance were very important as the police were considered symbols of The Bahamas to be admired and photographed by visitors. We could not waiver from the dress code, and there were regular inspections by the sergeants and station officers before we went on patrol.

In addition to being properly dressed, we had to be well-groomed and possess all the stipulated accoutrements - a pocket book, pencil, whistle and chain, and baton. At night we had to carry a flashlight, and on rainy days a cape or raincoat.

Rain did not stop police patrols back then. On Bay Street and the adjacent streets there were the regular patrol beats - we used bicycles or our feet, which made fitness so important. Inspection before leaving the station included shoes, beard, haircut and body odour. Patrols were briefed on incidents that had occurred on previous shifts, and advised of matters to give special attention to. A corporal would periodically check on the patrols to ensure that officers were on the alert.

The police force had two divisions - A and B - as well as the Traffic Section, the Fire Branch and the Criminal Investigation Department. A policeman's 24-hour day started at 10 am, when the division about to go on duty paraded in front of headquarters for inspection and assignments to the police stations. Disciplinary action would be taken if one was not properly attired or lacked the required accoutrements.

This meant an immediate hearing before the commissioner or his deputy. Penalties ranged from fines and revocation of time off to detention, and the commissioner could also impose prison sentences. The Main Guard at headquarters had a sentry in place, and a sentry was also provided at Government House. The march to and from Government

House with the heavy old .303 rifles was tiring, but as I said policemen were physically fit in those days.

Each police station had beds for officers to use when not on patrol or station duty. We had to carry a small suitcase with brass polish, brushes and all the necessary items for maintaining our uniform, as well as items for personal grooming. During the day we wore helmets and at night we wore caps. We worked for two-hour periods from 10am to 8pm, and four-hour periods from 8pm to 4am.

Handcuffs were of the screw type, which an officer could only put in place if the person being arrested was willing to cooperate. There were no hand radios. Officers making arrests were expected to take the person into custody by themselves, or find a telephone to call for help. There was resistance at times from prisoners, and even assaults, but that was to the peril of the prisoner as magistrates did not go lightly on those who resisted or assaulted policemen. Resistance usually resulted in a jail sentence.

Kit Inspection was a monthly parade when policemen had to present their uniforms and all accoutrements received from the police stores for inspection. This took place on Saturdays , and the cost of any missing kit would be deducted from our wages. To escape kit inspection, policemen often made arrests on Friday nights so they could attend court on Saturday mornings. Court attendance took priority over kit inspection.

Wages for constables in the early 1950s were two pounds and fifteen shillings per week. Of that sum we paid two pounds ten shillings for food. There was an allowance of 15 pounds per month. Our tunics were collected by John Chea every week. The cost of living was low back then, but needless to say these wages did not attract better educated Bahamians, who showed no interest in joining the police force. Even hotel workers made more money than we did.

Policemen attending court on their off-duty hours received no compensation or time back. Very often officers were assigned to work 12-hour shifts without any form of compensation. Personnel in the Criminal Investigation Department worked 60 hours per week in the day time, with one day off. The night shift was an 84-hour week, consisting of 12 hours each night from to 9pm to 9am, with no day off. Policemen could not leave their stations or vehicles without headdress, and smoking was strictly forbidden in the stations.

Wearing part of the uniform in public was a major disciplinary infraction. Policemen were required to salute senior officers from the rank of chief inspector upwards, as well as the police doctor, judges, magistrates and members of parliament. We had to be able to identify all parliamentarians in order to salute them.

Attending court was a form of parade and you had to dress properly. Caps were required in the magistrate's court, but helmets had to be worn in the supreme court. Good note-taking was important as prosecutors expected us to refer to our notes when testifying about measurements, descriptions and a host of other things where exact evidence was critical. For this reason policemen were required to keep their notebooks in good order and submit them regularly to the station officers for inspection.

In my years of service as a detective I learned how important it was to make notes during the investigation of crimes. Records of incidents or conversations that had taken place months or even years before could be of the utmost importance when testifying before the courts. Prosecutors always expressed admiration for my testimonial skills and the deft use of my pocket notebook. Eugene Dupuch once told me he was never happy having to cross-examine me as I was always ready with my notebook. I took it as a compliment. I remember wielding my notebook with great effect when testifying in the sedition case against Randol Fawkes, and in the Stokes Thompson murder trial. The notebook will always be an effective tool for police officers.

In my 25 years at CID we used a diary to record every activity, instruction, arrest, release, attorney visit and duty cycle. It could be mined by researchers, and was sometimes used as an exhibit in the courts. There was also the crime book, in which all incidents were reported, with entries of arrests made in red ink. The crime book was checked daily by the head of CID, who often added his directions for the investigating officers. There was also a duty book, a court book and a vehicle register. The functions performed by these books are all handled by computers today.

My initial attachment to CID was for a probation period of six months, after which I was assessed by Salathial Thompson and Albert Miller, who were very tough on me going through everything I wrote, even the times I reported on, and off duty. But in the end I received an outstanding report, which I did not really expect. In fact, I cried in private when I saw the report.

Detectives at CID were engaged in intelligence work, fraud investigations, VIP protection and drug interdiction. There was no separate drug squad at that time. Indeed, many Family Islands had no regular policemen at all, so detectives had to travel to the islands to investigate crimes, which were a rare occurrence in those days.

I enjoyed going to the islands and was often assigned to these cases after I had developed a good record of detection. I usually stayed with the local or district constable and ate what he offered gratis. I recall one visit to Long Island when I spent the night alone in a church at Clarence Town with an adjacent cemetery. I did not sleep that night.

To get to the islands we travelled by mailboat, and while there we used dinghy boats to travel between settlements. I have visited every settlement on Andros by dinghy boat, but Eleuthera and Bimini were my favourite destinations. Bimini was most entertaining during the big game fishing season and there was an adventure in every settlement on Eleuthera.

My record for good results in criminal investigations was due to several factors. First, I was good at making friends. Second, I used humour to obtain critical information. I could also keep the names of my informants confidential. And I was lucky to have a cordial relationship with the press, especially The Tribune and the Nassau Guardian. Their news reporting on major cases certainly helped my career.

Over the years, the Royal Bahamas Police Force has developed into a modern organization. Cars have replaced bicycles, computers have replaced registers, radio communication has replaced telephones and whistles, and the firearm has replaced the baton. Even the handcuffs are modern. But the old military discipline is no longer apparent among the rank and file today as it once was.

There is one piece of advice that I would pass on to younger officers. Although the police must support the policies of the government of the day, officers should never get involved in political issues. They should not take political sides, and should never disclose police business to politicians. This was the general situation when I was recruited, but when Lynden Pindling and the Progressive Liberal Party were elected for the first time in 1967, many of us were strongly sympathetic to the new regime and there was widespread discussion of what we could do to promote social change, which was so badly needed at the time.

Anthony Fields was the major organiser of secret communications promoting the PLP, and I was involved to a lesser extent. In fact, before Pindling won the government Fields got into trouble at Inagua when he was accused of campaigning for the PLP. My efforts were more subtle, but I too had strong feelings about majority rule. The police barracks with its 200 votes was a big threat to the City seats held by Sir Stafford Sands and Dr Raymond Sawyer, and was eventually removed from their constituencies. Our feelings were motivated by the racial discrimination that prevailed in the country at that time, as well as the general treatment of black policemen as second class citizens by the pre-1967 political leaders.

For example, I could not understand why British officers were provided with free housing, utilities and vehicles while Bahamian officers had to pay for all these things. And it was objectionable and cruel to have policemen working at the homes of government ministers without access to toilets or drinking water. But after the 1984 Commission of Inquiry on drug trafficking, I revoked my support for the PLP.

One of the major assets to investigations in the old days was our ability to conduct covert operations with international agencies without the knowledge of politicians. It has always been my view that police operations, in particular those involving international law enforcement agencies, should never be divulged to politicians until afterwards. Any police activity ought to remain secret because leaks could jeopardise the mission and endanger the safety of those involved.

Salathial Thompson, when he was commissioner, would always say that he did not want to know what crime-fighting operations were taking place. He just wanted to know the results. He refused to allow the police minister to go on vehicle patrols with officers, and once instructed me to execute a search warrant on the home of a member of parliament, who had not renewed his firearms licence for two years and who had rebuked us when we called about it.

A commissioner must always have the courage to decline requests from politicians that contravene good policy. This is one of the reasons why tenure is such an important issue. A commissioner must be able to perform his duties fairly and lawfully, without fear or favour.

CHAPTER 23

Carnival

In my early years at Cunupia village I did not have much exposure to the yearly carnival celebrations in Trinidad's cities. It was not until I moved to Port of Spain in 1943 that I began to enjoy this cultural event. But when I was recruited by the Royal Bahamas Police Force in 1952 I left Trinidad for good.

As my police career developed I turned into a workaholic. I neglected my family, the sports that I loved to play, and even my health. The excitement of crime fighting consumed me. During these years I was fortunate to meet and befriend two FBI agents - Gerry Forrester and Tom Dowd. They had observed my total immersion in my work and were concerned about it. On one visit to Miami, Forrester suggested that I get a medical check-up at a clinic used by FBI agents for their check-ups. The doctor advised me about the dangers of stress and said I had to find ways to leave my work behind occasionally. Back in Nassau a local doctor concurred with this advice, so I started going home and watching television during lunch hours.

I also began playing table tennis and tennis again in the evenings, and I officiated as a football referee on weekends. Eventually I found myself sleeping better and had more energy for my hours of work. Around this time there was a group travelling to Trinidad for carnival led by a former policeman named Eugene Edwards. They invited me to come along, and since I had always been a fan of calypso music, in 1969 I decided to take my vacation in Trinidad. It was the first time I had been home for carnival in 10 years.

That same year Prime Minister Lynden Pindling and a large Bahamian entourage also attended carnival. My homecoming was the best vacation I had experienced in years, and ever since I have continued my annual visits for carnival. Many Bahamians visit Trinidad for this event and some even take part in it regularly.

Scientists have confirmed that music bypasses the conscious mind and works with the body to reduce stress and susceptibility to disease. That's why my vacations are timed for carnival every year. It is just what the doctor ordered. On each visit I go to places that I had never seen during the 23 years that I spent in Trinidad as a youth. I also get together with relatives and schoolmates for many pleasant reunions.

Although my experience with carnival while growing up in Trinidad was limited, it has been rightly called "the greatest show on earth". It begins just after New Year's Day and continues until Ash Wednesday. But carnival is not only the masquerade parades. There are endless parties (known as fêtes) where you can dance to the music of the season performed by top soca artists.

Every year there is new music written especially for carnival that is danced to in wild abandon. Visitors soon learn to "wine" like the Trinis do, a term which means gyrating your hips to the beat of the music. There are inexpensive public fêtes attended by the masses together with upscale fêtes where the price of admission gets you all you want in premium drinks and foods, as well as the best music in the world.

These fêtes are important as they help to prepare carnival-goers for the hectic two days of the street parades. This is where you find out if you have what it takes to operate with little sleep and deal with party after party. In fact, many Trinis prepare for carnival by running miles each day to get their bodies in shape.

By far the best part of these vacations are the visits to the steel pan yards to listen to the new music being rehearsed for presentation at the great "Panorama" competitions. The winning band earns a first prize of one million T&T dollars. At the "Mas Camps" you can see the elaborate costumes being constructed, and at the renowned "Breakfast Shed" near the docks you can fill up with native foods and drinks.

These small restaurants in the Shed are very similar to the fish fry on Arawak Cay, and they attract many hotel tourists. The Breakfast Shed was originally built to cater to the stevedores and other dock workers, but it has become the favourite eating place of Trinidad's political and business elite. It consists of several kitchens under one roof with dining space along the waterfront. The kitchens are operated by elderly entrepreneurs who are experts in preparing traditional Trini dishes like curried crab and dumplings, brown stew chicken, fish broth, cow heel soup, or callaloo with crab and pig tail.

Carnival is now big business. It even caters to other carnivals that have sprung up around the world - Notting Hill in England; Brooklyn, Washington D.C., Atlanta, Orlando and Miami in the United States; or Toronto and Montreal in Canada. Wherever large groups of Trinis have emigrated there is likely to be a carnival, with non-stop partying for weeks

The music of carnival can be heard around the West Indies, played by big bands, as well as by local groups such as "Visage" in The Bahamas. Byron Lee and the Dragonaires of Jamaica took this music to the world stage when they began touring Europe, Asia, Africa, and North America decades ago. In fact, it was Byron Lee who called Trinidad & Tobago "the University of Culture". This diverse culture is derived from the many different ethnic groups that call Trinidad home - Africans, East Indians, Chinese, Arabs, Amerindians and Europeans.

Trinis pronounce the word "carnaval", but the older folks call it "camboulay", while the French creoles refer to it as "de mas." Whatever the name, I certainly agree that it is the world's greatest cultural celebration.

APPENDIX 1

On Illegal Immigration and Terrorism

Immigration is a very sensitive issue in The Bahamas. And illegal immigration has been a major problem for governments over the past several decades.

Public concern has always focused on the potential loss of jobs and the disproportionate use of public services by those who pay few taxes. But illegals are also blamed for rising crime rates, the spread of infectious diseases, and the cost of detention and repatriation. But there is another concern that ought to be uppermost in the minds of Bahamians; and that is the danger of terrorism.

A terrorist is someone who is ideologically inspired to unlawfully use force or violence against people or property to further their political or social objectives. They are trained to blend in and assimilate to their surroundings. Their activities are usually well-planned and well-organised, often striking at government or civilian targets in an effort to instil fear in the population at large.

It is important for a terrorist to arrive in a country unidentified and undocumented. And in The Bahamas there is an illegal population of tens of thousands of undocumented aliens. They live and work on most islands and we do not know who they are. There is no register of names, no photographs and no fingerprint data. During the 2011 earthquake, for example, hundreds of dangerous criminals escaped from Haitian prisons, but the Bahamian police never received any official information about these escapees, who included killers and rapists as well as political prisoners.

Terrorists must have the desire, ability and opportunity to commit a terrorist attack. In the modern era most terror attacks are directed at American citizens or property. This means that cruise ships, hotels and tourists in The Bahamas are potential targets. There are often more Americans berthed at the Prince George Wharf than there were in the World Trade Centre on September 11 2001. We cannot control the desire or ability to commit a terrorist act, but we can limit the opportunity, by protecting our borders and monitoring criminal activity. There must be a zero tolerance approach to our illegal immigration problem. The enemy may be living amongst us.

Over the years I have been able to discuss this issue with government ministers and senior law officers. I have also written commentaries for the newspapers. In the following paragraphs I outline some of the recommendations I have made over the past decade.

Identity Cards

Legislation should require the possession of identity cards by all immigrants, in place of a work permit. In addition to basic information, these wallet-sized cards should carry a photograph and a thumb or forefinger print. Immigrants with a clean police record who are born in The Bahamas should have some form of residential status allowing them to work. Cardholders would have to prove the payment of National Insurance fees and other taxes in order to have the card renewed, and the cards would have to be available at all times for inspection by law officers. A card would have to be presented at government clinics to obtain treatment and landlords would only be able to rent accommodation to cardholders. A moratorium would be held for illegal immigrants to register for the new identity cards, and anyone found without such a card would be liable to deportation.

Immigration Department

The number of immigration officers should be increased so that there is sufficient personnel for round-the-clock shifts. Communications equipment for these officers should be upgraded and the Immigration Department's activities should be more closely integrated with other law enforcement agencies. Money should be provided to pay for tips and develop confidential sources, and immigration officers should have the power to seize vehicles, vessels and equipment used in the transportation of illegal immigrants. The detention centre should be made more secure with improved fencing and surveillance cameras, and a second detention centre should be built at Inagua to house migrants picked up at sea. Officers should maintain accurate records of all those who breach the immigration laws, including photos and fingerprints. Deportees who return to The Bahamas should face criminal penalties if caught, and the captains and crews of all vessels found to be involved in human trafficking should be prosecuted to the full extent of the law.

Squatter Settlements

Measures should be taken to eliminate shanty towns wherever they exist. Squatters should be given written notice to vacate their premises, after which they would be forcibly evicted and the properties destroyed. Illegal migrants in The Bahamas are involved in a range of criminal activities, such as gambling, smuggling of drugs and guns, human trafficking and prostitution. Whenever illegals are arrested they should be questioned by security and intelligence officers to gain as much information as possible on these activities.

International Co-operation

The Bahamas should seek to co-operate with the Haitian and American governments on the implementation of new measures to prevent human trafficking. These could include rewards to Haitian nationals for information, soliciting the support of Haitian law enforcement agencies, and the possibility of joint patrols of the sea lanes around Haiti to apprehend and turn around vessels carrying illegal migrants. All such vessels should be searched for any type of contraband. Many Haitians who arrive in The Bahamas illegally are actually in transit to the United States, and it would be easy for terrorists to use the boats and the routes established by the traffickers.

APPENDIX 2

On Crime and Capital Punishment

Nothing disheartens and discourages police officers more than the knowledge that their efforts in apprehending criminals are too often no more than useless expenditures of time and effort. Unwarranted leniency in the form of bail, long adjournments, and other decisions frequently make a mockery of good police work. While we must strive to rehabilitate those who have strayed from lawful ways, we must also protect society from depraved individuals with no respect for law and order or the rights of others.

The scales of justice must be balanced.

Today our police officers are engaged in a war against young and not so young terrorists, who are determined to destroy the economy and force the rest of us to live in fear. They strike at government and civilian targets in an effort to instil that fear. The use of force or violence against people or property to further their own social objectives. Our law enforcement officers are constantly exposed to serious harm and death as they endeavour to maintain law and order. Even in the most minor situations they find themselves exposed to the deadly force of firearms in the hands of thugs who kill to make good their escape from capture. And our residents and visitors are exposed to the danger of gunfire should they find themselves in the area of battle.

There are those persons among us who frequently criticise police officers, who are forced to use firearms in the course of their duty and for their own protection. They have mere seconds to decide on a course of action, but in most instances police officers shoot to live, not to kill. Crimes of violence in our country threaten our peaceful way of life. In most instances the weapon of choice is a gun and it is essential that we do all that we can to rid ourselves of the menace of firearms. In many cases, the types of gun used is similar to those used by terrorists around the world, and our police officers are doing a remarkable job apprehending criminals with guns and recovering illegal weapons.

Inveterate criminals who prey on honest folk and succeed in escaping punishment are encouraged in their disdain for law and go on to commit depredations of even more heinous proportions. For a peaceful and wholesome society, it is imperative that the rights of law-abiding citizens be given the same respect and consideration as the rights of criminals, whose vicious deeds have resulted in untold suffering. Yet attorneys are able to get long adjournments in the courts and delay proceedings almost indefinitely. These delays give criminals the upper hand as very often witnesses forget the details of their testimony, and the criminals also have time to threaten or bribe witnesses, who will often disappear or change their testimony at trial.

Police brutality is one of the common ploys used by defence attorneys. It has been used for decades throughout the world and will continue to be used to have written confessions made by accused criminals thrown out in court, or to influence jury decisions. Police Officers, in particular those who are involved in the investigation of crime, are provided with training and administrative directions on interrogation and the taking of statements. Statements of admissions are to be taken under caution on a prescribed form; with start and end times recorded. The words used by the suspect are not to be reconstructed, and each page of the statement must be signed after it is read over to the suspect or read by him. A copy must also be provided to the suspect on request.

Persons held in custody must also be advised of available facilities, such as toilets and refreshments, as well as their right to call a relative or an attorney. There are conditions under which an attorney may not be made available immediately - for example, the need to search a suspect's home for evidence - because allowing such communication could defeat the purpose of the investigation. An attorney may also encounter delays in meeting with clients that are being held by police if it is possible that his presence may affect the outcome of an investigation. There are also the Judges' Rules, a guide to police investigators. These rules confirm that, at any stage of an investigation, a suspect should be able to consult privately with an attorney, provided that in such case no unreasonable delay or hindrance is caused to the processes of the investigation or the administration of justice.

As soon as a police officer has reasonable grounds for suspecting that a person has committed a crime, he must caution that person before questioning him. In The Bahamas the caution is as follows: "You are not obliged to say anything unless you wish to do so, but what you say may be put in writing and given in evidence". It would be seen that these rules, which apply in England and Wales, are designed to secure that only voluntary answers and statements are admitted in evidence.

The police must follow certain regulations when persons are arrested. There must be a record of the arrest, the place of custody, the times in and out for whatever reason, the names of officers taking the person out, and the times of feeding and visitation. There is sufficient opportunity for suspects to complain promptly about brutal treatment, and our police officers, in particular those involved in the investigation of serious crimes, are familiar with the contents of the Judges' Rules and Force Regulations. Clearly, from all of the above, there is a vast amount of protection given to criminals. In fact, their rights far exceed the rights of victims.

The question of capital punishment has been a controversial issue in The Bahamas and throughout the English-speaking Caribbean. This issue has generated huge quantities of written and spoken words, as well as frequent demonstrations by supporters of the death penalty. The struggle for answers concerning the taking of another life is one in which every Bahamian should lend a voice. In a democracy such as ours, this is not an issue for a handful of men to decide alone. As a former law enforcement officer, it is my belief that a great many of those who are opposed to capital punishment emanate from those areas of our society that are protected from the horrors that human beings can perpetrate against their fellows.

Searching thought must be given before any mandatory decision to carry out capital punishment in every case of murder. At the same time, nothing is so precious in our Bahamas and Caribbean as the life of a human being, whether a criminal or not. There must be the legal safeguards, which our societies demand. Experience has clearly demonstrated that the time-proven deterrents to crime are sure detection, swift apprehension and proper punishment. Each is a necessary ingredient to the mix. Law-abiding citizens have a right to expect that the efforts of law officers in detecting and apprehending criminals will be followed by realistic punishment. There can be no doubt of the sincerity of many of those who deplore capital punishment, but a realistic approach to the problem demands that they weigh the right of persons to live their lives free from fear of killers. As a policeman, I always thought of capital punishment as a lighthouse. How many ships would have run aground if it was not there? And how many people are not on death row because of the deterrent effect of executions?

In 1958 during my training at the West Riding Detective School in Yorkshire, capital punishment was still on the books in Britain. There was capital murder and murder. Murders that warranted the death penalty included those committed in furtherance of a crime or while trying to escape lawful custody, and those committed by the use of explosives or poison. Person who committed treason, or who killed a law officer in the execution of his duty or who committed a second murder were also subject to hanging.

In my humble view - one that is shared by many in the region - the Privy Council in London will continue to obstruct hangings in former British territories in support of the European effort to abolish capital punishment. Like many others, I am disappointed that The Bahamas and some countries in the Caribbean still cling to the Privy Council of England as the court of last resort, despite being independent for decades. The Bahamas is a part of CARICOM, where the Caribbean Court of Justice is the final court of appeal. As far as I am aware, we contribute financially to such regional initiatives, and we have proven that we have the moral and intellectual capacity to run our own nations. However, we do not seem to have faith that we can judge ourselves. We appear to be unwilling to take responsibility for our jurisprudential self-determination. The British parliament has indicated that the judicial services provided to former colonies by the Privy Council are a burden on the British taxpayers. It is also well known that the law lords in London have commended Caribbean judges on judgements they have delivered and have repeatedly stated that these judges are better suited to deliberate on regional matters. In order to be a fair Judge, one must take account of the historical and cultural background of those who are being judged. A British judge can be challenged to understand our behaviour within its social context. In my opinion, if The Bahamas would become a part of the CCJ judicial appeals would be more expeditiously dealt with and less costly for participants.

There are two sides to every story - and that includes the death penalty, which has sparked a very emotional debate involving law, politics, religion and morality. Those in favour of the death penalty take the view that there is no need to discuss whether hanging is good or bad, or whether it will be a deterrent to crime, because it is the law and has always been the law. According to this view, the only issue is enforcement. There does not appear to be much opposition to the death penalty amongst Bahamian politicians, and many MPs who would likely shout "hang them high." The debate therefore should centre on how to remove the legal obstacles to carrying out executions.

In 1993 the Pratt & Morgan judgement ruled that condemned prisoners should not be kept on death row for more than five years. After reading the 2011 Privy Council judgement overturning the death sentence of convicted murderer Max Tido, I am convinced that the British law lords will never make any ruling in support of the death penalty. Delays in executions are engineered by clever lawyers in an "endless journey to stall the process". Appeals are made to local courts, the Privy Council and to international human rights bodies, and these delaying tactics then become grounds for not carrying out the sentence. The chief function of parliament is to legislate, so it must introduce laws that can prevent convicted murderers from using legal strategies to avoid execution. There ought to be at least two categories of murder. The death penalty should be mandatory for murder one, or capital murder, and time limits should be imposed on the appeals process.

In the Max Tido case, the Privy Council said there was "overwhelming" evidence against the defendant, so "a finding of guilt was inevitable". Tido was found guilty in 2006 of the murder of 16-year-old Donnella Conover after testimony that the teenager was lured from her home in the early morning hours of May 2, 2002, and brutally beaten to death off Cowpen Road. This was a heinous and gruesome crime, which left relatives and friends of the victim in a state of permanent shock, but the Privy Council did not think it was heinous enough to warrant Tido's execution. And as long as we have the Privy Council as a final court of appeal, there will be no hangings in The Bahamas.

APPENDIX 3

Statement to the 1984 Commission of Inquiry

I was born in Trinidad on the 19th July, 1927, and resided there until March, 1951 when I joined the Royal Bahamas Police Force. I was recruited in Trinidad with 16 others for the Police Force here. In March 1981 I retired from the Police Service and joined Resorts International Inc. as their Security Advisor.

During my term of office in the police force I was the recipient of several training courses at home and abroad. Most significant among these were the Detective Training School in West riding, Yorkshire, the Scottish Police College in Edinburgh, and INTER-POL in Paris. In addition to the above I have attended numerous training seminars held locally and overseas. Of the 30 years of service in the police force, 25 were spent in the Criminal Investigation Department, where I started my career as a detective constable in June 1952 and became Assistant Commissioner (CID) in 1970.

I am proud of the record of the police force and my accomplishments during my service. I will always be very grateful to the force, the government and the people of the Bahamas for providing me with the opportunities to improve myself in the career of my choice.

All of the information I propose to give in this statement may be considered rel-evant to paragraph (b) , (c) and (d), of the Commission's terms of reference. I have no information on paragraph (a), except for my suspicions of corruption on the police force, which has been proven in numerous cases where police officers and other civil servants have been involved in the drug traffic. During my years of service in the force, in particular those years spent in the gazetted ranks, I have never received any information from anyone pertaining to corruption of government ministers or members of parlia-ment acquiescing or participating in any activities promoting or facilitating the trans-shipment of dangerous drugs.

During the late 1950s and early 1960s, as I moved into the senior ranks, I met and worked with several officers from overseas, in particular from the USA. Apart from the working relationship, which was excellent, I also developed a personal relationship with many of them. There was mutual trust, a desire to help and learn from each other the varying techniques of the profession. But most of all, I was able to develop a close friend-ship with them and learned quite a lot about policing. I worked very closely with agents of the FBI, DEA, US Customs, the US Secret Service and the Treasury Department, and also with police personnel in Canada, Jamaica, Bermuda, Haiti, Trinidad & Tobago, and several other Caribbean countries.

The relationship worked well for our police. The exchange of information and ideas, providing literature for training, and even arranging training courses were some of the benefits derived from the relationship. Most important was the type of international co-operation which circumvented red tape and enabled all of us to get the job done expeditiously and in confidence.

Prior to the 1960s, drug abuse in the Commonwealth of the Bahamas had been confined mainly to possession and use of ganja. Trafficking had been minimal and the persons involved were mostly foreigners - Americans and Jamaicans. The statistics in the Police Annual Reports for the early 60s will show that there had been a steady rise in the number of Bahamians being arrested for drug offences, and the problem became more serious as ganja became identifiable with the cult known as the rastafarians, whose adherents considered its use complementary to their religious beliefs. The cult was spreading slowly in the Bahamas, where over-employment existed and Jamaican nationals were arriving here in large numbers for work. As our country grew more prosperous, drug trafficking and related crimes became more sophisticated. Improvised packages of ganja began to be detected by Customs officials at the Nassau International Airport, and to a lesser degree in Freeport, and at the local post offices.

In 1968 the Drug Squad was formed in the CID. I subsequently increased the number of personnel and changed the name to Serious Crime Drug Squad. I was satisfied that the increase in violent crimes in the country was associated with drugs. It must have been obvious to all police officers that we were in for some hard times. Drug abuse, firearms being frequently used in holdups, a vast increase in rapes and an appearance of lawlessness among the youth, should have convinced anyone that something had to be done with the police force and the law of the land. Yet frequent requests to police administrators to increase the strength of the CID and provide us with the equipment to fight this cancer in it's early stages apparently fell on deaf ears. My advice to the Commissioner of Police and his very senior officers was not being taken seriously.

At the start of the 1970s, the trafficking south of the US border in drugs between the cultivating and manufacturing countries in South and Central America, and the USA had been suppressed by US law enforcement agents in a prolonged operation called, "Intercept". The routes between the USA and Mexico were closed and an alternative route was necessary. Jamaica and the Bahamas had become transshipment ports. The harder drugs - cocaine, hashish, heroin etc - were being introduced. The geographical position of the Bahamas with its vast archipelago and total land area of about 5,400 square miles of islands varying in size made it ideally suitable as a transit point between the countries in South and Central America and the USA, and was therefore prone to be a haven for the runners. The task of providing even superficial police coverage throughout the Bahamas stretched resources to the limit. Statistics for 1972 will show that of the 273 persons arrested for drug offences, 76 were Bahamians. Of the 306 persons arrested in 1974, 146 were Bahamians.

By this time the police were receiving support and collaboration from law enforcement agencies in the US and Jamaica. There were information exchanges, undercover investigations, joint surveillance exercises, air and sea patrols, and electronic surveillance of certain landing strips. The DEA provided training for police, Customs and Immigration officers, both here and at schools in the US. Our police co-operated with the DEA in this area. However, there were two requests made to us by the DEA which were declined. At separate meetings between DEA officials and our police administrators, the then Commissioner of Police and the DEA asked for permission to use our police radio frequency when operating in the Bahamas so that they could communicate with our personnel directly by radio when on sea and air patrol. The request was denied. The DEA also suggested that all uncharted airstrips on those Islands used by aircraft transporting drugs be damaged by blowing large holes with explosives. The DEA offered to provide the equipment and expertise. The request was denied.

At that time Mr Salathial Thompson was the Commissioner of Police. He had been appointed to the post in 1973. We had expected vast improvements from him in modernizing the force, and improving working conditions. We knew that the government had a lot of faith in him and it was our opinion that he would be able to get things done. The force needed a "shot-in-the arm" and we thought this was the man who could provide it. The decisions made in response to the DEA's request created some doubt in my mind about the type of administration I expected.

In the early 1970s I was transferred from the CID to the Uniform Branch where I acted as Assistant Commissioner in charge of the New Providence District and the Family Islands. I was later transferred to Freeport, Grand Bahama as officer in charge of that district. In 1974 I was returned to New Providence, where I became Assistant Commissioner in charge of the CID. I immediately embarked upon a programme to strengthen relations with foreign law enforcement agencies, in particular US Customs and the DEA. The response and the subsequent results were excellent.

In the CID we observed that the crime trend had continued. Firearms were frequently used in robberies, rapes and other violent crimes were on the increase. We were satisfied that many of these crimes perpetrated by juveniles and young adults were drug related. We had made it our business to question youths arrested about drug abuse and in most cases they were admittedly "high" when committing crimes. In the CID the cases per man were exceedingly high, the working hours exceedingly long, and the general conditions in the offices deplorable. These conditions were having an adverse effect on the CID. Detectives were short-cutting investigations, resulting in poor presentation of evidence in the courts. There were numerous accusations of police brutality, and several accidents due to tiredness and long working hours. Police Headquarters, through my reports, was made aware of these problems. In fact, I had discussed manpower needs with some of the senior CID officers and made recommendations to the Commissioner.

No reply was ever forthcoming. The Serious Crime and Drug Squad was overworked. This affected our ability and commitment to deal with the drug problem. Administrators appeared to be unconcerned about the escalation in crime and the drug traffic. It appeared that top priority was being given to the needs of the Security and

Intelligence Branch, where some of the best investigating officers were being posted. The CID lost top personnel to that Branch, whose duties included VIP security, political and civil investigations. I never saw the need for such a large SIB staff. The Bahamas is a peaceful country with no civil unrest, and the government of the day is the popular choice. It was always my opinion that crime and drug trafficking should have been given top priority. I was very vocal at senior officers' conferences about these matters. Police Headquarters eventually abandoned the idea of the conferences which had been going on for several years.

In March 1975 I was selected to attend the Interpol Caribbean Conference in Kingston, Jamaica. It was my hope that this report would have convinced the police administrators of the need to effectively increase the strength of the CID and to improve our communication with other police forces in the area. My presence at the conference helped to improve my relationship with other police officers from various countries.

During these years, as the drug traffic grew, the need for joint undercover operations was necessary if we were to arrest major offenders. The head of the DEA in Miami was interested in assisting. Undercover operations arranged by us in the past had been very rewarding, resulting in several arrests and the seizure of large quantities of drugs. The success of undercover operations depends a great deal on secrecy and speed. It would be a dangerous exercise if such matters had to go through the administrative red tape of other departments. Too many persons are likely to know of the operations and there could be leaks.

As a result of the escalation of the drug traffic, we were making large seizures of tons of ganja in the Islands. The large loads were being brought to Nassau for storage and subsequent destruction. The drugs were stored in old buildings in the headquarters compound and later at Oakes Field. These buildings were the targets of those who were obviously involved with police officers in stealing of drugs from these unsuitable premises. After the first attack on one of the buildings I suggested to Police Headquarters that I place a select team of armed detectives to maintain surveillance on the buildings to capture the burglars. I was satisfied that police personnel were involved. My request was denied. The Commissioner instructed that uniformed officers be posted at the buildings.

The theft of large quantities of ganja continues. We lost a lot of respect from the public during this period. The DEA had offered to have the large seizures taken to Miami by a Coast Guard cutter to be destroyed. This offer was declined. Our senior officers were of the opinion that the DEA did not trust us. I was all for it as I was aware of the amount of work involved in the destruction of ganja. This was being done by serious crime personnel who could be doing other work instead. I had requested the purchase of an incinerator for burning the ganja. I never got it. I recommended that we ask government to provide us with the old Customs warehouse building on East Street as a storage place. The plan was to renovate the building, strengthening the ceiling, closing up the doors on the roadside and cutting an entrance inside the police compound. I had asked that alarms be installed that would signal in the Police Radio Control Room and the Quarter Guard. This plan would have eliminated the need for police officers to watch the drugs and the temptation of corruption in that area would have been eliminated.

The building was being used by the Ministry of Education. We never got the use of the building. The theft of drugs from police storage areas continues.

From the mid 1970s onward the transit traffic grew. Ship and aircraft used our Islands and cays at regular intervals for refuelling and for storage. Among the Islands being used were Mayaguana, Inagua, Bimini, Andros, the Berry Islands, the Exuma Cays, Cat Island, Acklins, and the infamous Gorda Cay in the Abacos. Drug wars had started between local residents who began stealing shipments from the runners. High-powered automatic weapons were being used. There were a number of drug-related murders and gangland-style killings. The local residents involved purchased high-powered boats and guns. Sea piracy became a new type of drug-related crime.

Bimini was the worst of the Islands. There was evidence of police corruption there and the population seemed to favour the trafficking. Several prominent persons were arrested in a raid to that Island led by me. When we were leaving with the prisoners, rocks were thrown at us by adults as well as children. The raid was a success due to the use of Defence Force equipment and complete secrecy. The team was not told where we were headed until late at night at sea. Information on police movements was rewarded by the smugglers. The charter of a plane or boat by the police touched off a network of messages to the criminals.

The Ministry of Home Affairs convened a meeting to discuss law enforcement action to 'close down' Bimini. The meeting was attended by Customs, Immigration, Police and other officials of government. A Permanent Secretary chaired the meeting. We produced a plan which I am told was for the Cabinet. No more was heard about our plan. The cost would have been phenomenal, which apparently caused the lack of action.

Attached is a memorandum which I wrote to the Commissioner at his request in reply to a memo from the Ministry of Home Affairs. The information was for the U.N. Commission on Narcotic Drugs. In May 1979 I attended Interpol American Regional Conference in Bermuda along with Mr. Avery Ferguson the new ACP in charge of the CID. I have attached extracts from reports of that conference.

I have only visited Norman's Cay on one occasion. I was sent there by the Commissioner to see what was going on. There was information of transit traffic in drugs. Upon my return I reported that the infrastructure is there for such trafficking and the absence of any officers on the cay made it a haven for any type of smuggling. I knew that Joe Lehder owned the cay and I had seen a lot of latins on the cay. There were also a few Bahamians working there. I am unable to remember when I visited, but it may have been either after some disclosure was made by the DEA or by Mr. Norman Solomon.

In the last paragraph of my report I advised that government should consider having big investors coming to our Islands and cays provide buildings for police and Customs personnel at the start. I have seen Robert Vesco on occasions in Nassau. On one occasion I was asked to accompany an Immigration officer to deliver a letter to him. I have never heard of any involvement in drugs by Mr. Vesco.

Robert Vesco

For several years the police force used the laboratories of other police forces - the Jamaica Police, Dade Country Public Safety and the FBI. As the drug traffic grew, so did the demand for our own lab. We were eventually able to use a government lab in Nassau to analyse drugs. The police force recruited Mr. Carey at the rank of Inspector and sent him to the UK to study forensic science. While Mr. Carey was away I wrote to Police Headquarters, reminding them that we would need an equipped lab before his return. I had been lecturing regularly to the service clubs in Nassau and solicited their assistance in getting a lab for Mr. Carey. I told the Commissioner of the progress I made and a Mr. Jones visited him and told him that his club would be prepared to provided the funds for the equipment, provided that a suitable building could be found. The commissioner sent me to Miami to get prices and ideas on how to equip a lab. I returned with a full report from my friends in Dade County, but I heard no more about our lab. We could not produce a building and the club dropped the idea.

Mr. Carey returned with honours. Several years have passed and there is still not a lab. The analysis of drugs is creating hardships in getting cases completed before the courts. It would be interesting if the correct statistics could be obtained about the number of cases pending for months awaiting lab reports and the number that has been dismissed due to the lack of the lab report. One may find that Mr. Carey is being overworked and is frustrated by the lack of concern over providing him with proper facilities and recognition.

I have attached herewith documents of certain other recommendations made by me from time to time, which may be of interest. I am satisfied that the administration of the police force at that time had no intention of implementing any new ideas coming from its younger officers. Many of us were too scared to press for reforms or challenge any decisions made at Police Headquarters. I was subsequently branded as being disloyal because of my struggle to implement modern methods of policing and better working conditions. I am sure that government did not get any of these recommendations.

APPENDIX 4

1998 Comments on National Crime Commission Report

I wish to express my congratulations to the government for making the appointment, and to the Commission for a job well done in the limited time given to them. Secondly, I wish to state that there are parts of the reports with which I concur, there are comments in the report with which I disagree, and there are subjects discussed that required more study and additional information.

1.23. As an adjunct to the general necessity for community involvement in all aspects of the matters related to crime, Commissioners would emphasise the need for all persons to have a higher regard for their own security. Reasonable precautions would reduce opportunities for many crimes, thus minimising the work for an overextended police force.

In part 3, we point out that business owners should assume greater responsibility for the security of their premises and the safety of their customers rather than rely on the police force." I agree with the statement on crime prevention made by the commissioners. It is my opinion that they should have recommended that crime prevention efforts greatly increased through police communications, public education and intensified crime prevention programs by the media.

The funds for the crime prevention education drive should be part of the police budget and programs could be sponsored by the private sector. The crime prevention unit of the force should be given more time or even a program on Radio Bahamas to discuss crime prevention measures that can be taken by our citizens to protect themselves in the home and on the streets.

The major problem facing our society today is crime. The word alone conjures up images of gruesome killings, domestic violence, rapes, abductions, armed robberies and burglaries. We see a threat to our way of life and the safety and security of our loved ones and our property. It is therefore important that we encourage our citizens to take every precaution keeping in mind that criminals do not want to get caught and anything done that would improve the chances of them being caught is a plus for the war on crime.

The police must continue to use deadly force against criminals armed with deadly force against criminals armed with deadly weapons. There should be no question about this fact. The law provides for the use of deadly force and advises when such force must be used.

2.3.5. I concur with the commissioners views on a curfew for young persons. It would not achieve the purpose of reducing crime, it is unconstitutional to restrict the movement of persons over the age of 18 years and it would create more problems for the police to enforce such a curfew.

Sports has long been demonstrated as a means of directing the energies of the young to acceptable ends. Part of the answer lies in the formation of clubs as opposed to teams. Remember the days of the clubs, such as St. Agnes, St. Bernards, the Vikings, St Albans, the Setons, the Pedal Pushers, St. Georges, the Sea Scouts in which young and old met in doors and on the playing fields. Playing or consorting with the young were the role models and the community leaders. We must encourage this club atmosphere again.

2.3.11. I concur with the commissioners that roadside garages are; polluting the sub-soil, destinations for stolen vehicles or parts, but most importantly the environment is defaced by old abandoned vehicles, which tend to reduce the value of land and homes in those areas. The hundreds of abandoned vehicles are infested with rats and other pests. It would be very simple to eliminate roadside garages by assisting them to form cooperatives and providing crown lands for them in a particular area. Making them responsible for the cleanliness of the location.

3.4.5. We are all aware of the fact that trade unionists have a duty to ensure that the rights of workers are not compromised. I am aware of the fact that certain trade unionists when informed of thefts perpetrated by their members try to discourage court prosecution by making deals with the hotels. The worker may be fired, but will move elsewhere to work as there is no criminal record of conviction on file. Unions try to condone criminal offences perpetrated by their members.

4.2.3. It is not expected that our Defence Force would be placed on the street to fight crime, but they could be used to protect government buildings, residences of Heads of State and Ministers, the Ambassador and High Commissioner etc, thereby relieving trained police officers for the street duties. There has always been good cooperation between our law enforcement agencies. I cannot believe that such cooperation and understanding have degenerated to the state mentioned by the commissioners. It is necessary though for these law enforcement agencies to meet regularly and discuss strategies for reducing the flow of drugs and guns into New Providence and The Family Islands.

It must be of concern when vessels or vessels transporting illegal can reach New Providence undetected. The same may apply to drugs and guns. There is a need for full cooperation from U.S. government agencies in trying to trace the sources from where guns were purchased in the United States.

5.1.6. The commissioners were apparently not told that most of those officers enlisting in the force at the rank of Inspector have made remarkable progress and have made remarkable contributions to the force. Their education and technical knowledge have been assets. University graduates, in particular those with technical knowledge are needed.

3.3.10. To address the type of crimes perpetrated against farmers and fishermen the police must organise special patrols in the farm areas at certain times of the day and night when the thieves are leaving the farms on foot or in their vehicles with the loot to sell to those dishonest persons who purchase for resale. There must be proper harbour patrols to protect the boats moored at public docks. The Defence Force must be more involved in harbour patrols around New Providence. If the citizenry will desist from buying the bunches of stolen bananas and other produce, and inform the police about the thieves these crimes could be eradicated.

5.1.8. The statement indicating that CID Officers "tend to develop an arrogance based on their seemingly 'elite' status which adversely affects the harmonious working relationship with other branches, and some CID Officers tend to regard themselves as other than ordinary police officers are misleading. Persons giving such information to the commissioners may think themselves inferior. Of my 30 years in the force I was in the CID for 25 years. After leaving the force I continued with the police reserves in the CID. I am hearing of this so-called superiority complex for the first time. What I am aware of is the dedication displayed by CID. Officers, the vast knowledge they acquire through on the job training, reading and being present on crime scenes. The long hard hours they work and the challenges they encounter daily makes them an example, but not superior to others in the force. A CID officer arriving scene of a serious crime is expected to take over the investigation as he would be held responsible, but the uniform officer has a role to play and must do so. It is not to the force's benefit to transfer CID. Officers too often. It is a loss of a trained investigator to the crime-fighting machine. When the investigator goes his confidential informants are lost or have to be redeveloped to trust other officers.

5.1.17. It is a fact that the force is burdened with escort, guard and other court duties for which several police officers are deployed. Let us stop becoming 'Americanised' with talk of a marshall's office, etc. There are options which would be less costly, i.e. increase the prison staff and have them provide the escorts to the courts from the prison; increase the police establishment to provide personnel for the courts, and build a remand court at Fox Hill for the large percentage of prisoners that are presently transported all the way to Bank Lane just to be further remanded. It would be good if the cells in the basement of the court building could be renovated and re-activated. The Defence Force should be delegated with the responsibility to provide personnel for all those duties to be performed for cabinet ministers, heads of state and other dignitaries.

5.1.23. It appears that the most senior officer on duty at night is the duty officer in the control room. It has now become necessary for a very senior officer to be on duty at night - assistant commissioner or superintendent - to provide support on the ground and to be at the scene of serious crimes. I have always felt comfortable when my senior officer was around with me on night duty or available in an office where he could be readily contacted for advice.

5.1.25. I agree with the commissioners in not recruiting abroad. However, if it becomes impossible to find suitable recruits here it may become necessary to do so. Recruiting on contract with fixed salaries and repatriation at the end of the contract may be acceptable to most Bahamians. In the fifties local men did not want to join the force. Recruitment abroad was necessary and this was accepted by Bahamians. It must be noted that in many forces in the Commonwealth foreigners are recruited in limited numbers for special reasons.

5.1.31-33. Don't knock community policing and zero tolerance. One is good for public relations. Zero tolerance has been a big crime solver in cities such as New York, Chicago, Toronto, and Kingston, where the concept has been employed effectively. Our zero tolerance efforts here are far from effective. The basic things are not being done to make it effective. The motorcyclists are still riding without helmets and the trailers are still being drawn with-out lights or reflectors etc. While I agree that some police officers may be uncivil towards the youths sitting on the walls or walking the streets late at night, it is my opinion that it is necessary at this time to discourage the wall sitting and loitering, but the officers should be trained to deal with such matters in a civil manner. Removing them from the walls may be saving them from harm. As far as I am aware the "arbitrary" round-ups described in the report refer to arrests of persons suspected of committing crimes. These so-called round-ups have been successful in solving many crimes.

It is difficult to imagine why a magistrate mentioned in this paragraph as being a witness to police misconduct - "an unprovoked violent assault" on young men who were "doing nothing" - did not approaching the officers or did not report his observation to the commissioner.

5.1.38-39. The hiring of police officers by private persons or businesses is designed to relieve the force from having to deploy off-duty personnel to private functions with-out remuneration. It has been the consensus of opinion among members of the police force that those persons and businesses requiring police officers on duty at private functions ought to pay the force for the service. Private functions such as; parties, dances, concerts, boxing, wrestling and the carnivals requires extra numbers of police officers for crowd control etc. The promoters should pay a fee. Of course, application must be made to the commissioner for approval and the force command will select personnel from suitable locations bearing in mind the officers' regular work schedule, etc. All payments to be made to the force command for paying the officers concerned. The system of deploying off-duty officers for these extra duties without pay, which is decades old, must cease forthwith.

5.1.47. The commercial crime unit for years has been very efficient and effective. The team of officers there are dedicated. It is unfair to describe the officers as being weak in pursuing commercial crimes. The report should have described the weaknesses and if possible give examples. Many persons and business concerns in our communities in cases of fraud try to deal with such matters themselves and, failing to get satisfactory results, would then report the matter to the police. The delay creates problems for the police finding the suspect and quite often important evidence is no longer available. The public would read about bank frauds, insurance company frauds and large thefts from workers unions, but in the absence of complaints the police cannot act. In most complaints of fraud the complainants accountants or auditors provide all of the evidence for the investigators. All the investigator needs to know is what evidence is required and where to find it. The force budget could not afford lawyers or accountants, but may be able to assist commercial crime staff with courses.

5.3.15. It may not be popular with the commissioners to locate a maximum security prison outside of New Providence, but it would be ideal for security reasons. Why have a high security prison in our tourist mecca where the bulk of our population reside? There are scores of dangerous criminals at Fox Hill. It could be disastrous to our communities and our tourist industry if some of those murderers, who were on death row, escaped in this crowded city where recapture could take longer. The commissioners are apparently unaware of some of the vicious crimes perpetrated by some of those persons. There are at least two serial killers in our jail, one of whom has stated that he would kill again. On an Island in an isolated location security would be a lot better. It should be noted that maximum security prisons in most countries are in isolated locations. I submit that anywhere in The Bahamas prisoners would be able to maintain contact with their families.

Persons on the Family Islands maintain contact with inmates in Nassau now.

It is hoped that the contents of this document would be accepted as constructive end intended to enlighten the public and encourage reading and debate of the report.

APPENDIX 5

1999 Letter to the Prime Minister

Dear Sir,

Over the past months working with the Police I have been able to observe many of the existing problems, not only in the Force, but in other Law enforcement Agencies, which need to be recognized and immediate steps need to be taken to correct them if we are to make recognizable and adequate gains in the eradication of crime.

The response displayed by your Government in these few short years in office indicates that it is very committed to doing something about crime. The Police Force is now fairly well equipped, training is proceeding and morale has improved considerably. It is encouraging to note that in spite of all of the criticism and blame leveled at the Police by the media, and in particular the "talk shows", the Force continues to work diligently to maintain peace and good order in our society. I have no doubt judging from my close association with the rank and file that the Police efforts will continue and greater strides will be made in the coming months.

I have been making observations also of other areas where the lack of enforcement of regulations and rules eventually increase the burdens placed on the Police Force.

During the months of my employment as Force Training Officer I have taken the liberty to speak with many law enforcement officers about crime, to observe the work of the courts, to listen to the many problems and hurdles being experienced by the Police, to discuss with senior Police Officers the evident lack of motivation and the reluctance to deal with so many minor offences perpetrated on the streets of New Providence and several other crime related matters. I have written memoranda on "strategies to combat crime", which I am told have been well received throughout the Force.

The problems as I see them are now listed for review.

The Police Force

(a) Recruitment. The Force is experiencing great difficulty getting suitable applicants locally.

(b) Management and Supervision is lacking in certain areas.

The problem is mainly caused by the middle management group of officers, such as; Inspectors, Sergeants and Corporals.

(c) Discipline is lacking

(d) There are some social problems that need to be addressed.

P.O. Box SS-5179 • Nassau, N.P., Bahamas

Telephone: (242) 323-6115 or 325-4379 • Pager # (242) 381-1927

(e) communication with the media and publicizing excellent achievements of the Force is lacking. The public needs to know of the good work being done by the Police.

(f) crime prevention education and crime watch programs need to be 'improve. This could be done effectively through a weekly radio show hosted by the Police.

(g) failure to enforce the "zero tolerance" is hurting the reputation of the Force. The public needs to see 'an active effort being reduce minor crime on the streets.

I now turn to the other Government departments.

Road Traffic Department:

(a) Records in the department are not up-to-date and inefficiencies.

(b) Street signs (traffic) are down or not painted.

(c) Vehicle inspection needs improvement. With the escalation in stolen vehicles it is time to check serial numbers.

(d) More enforcement of regulations and rules pertaining to public transportation.

(e) A link between the Police and Road Traffic Computers would be an asset.

Immigration Department.

(a) Efficient management of records is required. The department should always be aware of persons who have overstayed the time of their visits.

(b) A link to Police computers is needed.

Customs Department

(a) Enforcement at our ports must be upgraded. Electronic equipment for detecting firearms etc. must be installed.

(b) Frequent dialogue with the Police is lacking.

(c) Joint surveillance exercises are needed.

Health & Environment Departments

(a) Health Inspectors are not checking food vendors, restaurant kitchens and other food outlets as often as they should.

(b) The laws regarding litter in yards and outside business houses are obviously not being enforced.

(c) Garbage toting vehicles being driven uncovered along our streets. No enforcement being seen.

(d) Dumping of garbage on private and public property continues.

(e) The law regarding undeveloped property is not being enforced.

Prisons

(a) A proper patrol system is sadly lacking. Electronic equipment needs to be installed to monitor the movement of prison guards on patrol.

(b) Discipline among guards is lacking. There is information that disciplinary charges laid against guards are seldom prosecuted.

(c) Corrupt practices exist.

Courts

(a) Bail continues to be a major problem for the Police.

(b) Attendance of witnesses. The non-attendance of witnesses, public and Police causes delays and accounts for congestion on the calendars.

(c) Justices of the Peace are not getting enough cases for trial.

(d) Better security needed for exhibits and case files.

(e) Electronic security and surveillance equipment required for the buildings.

(f) Case management in the Supreme Court system is causing many important and serious cases to reach trial years after the crime had been committed, which tends to give defence attorneys an advantage.

Attorney-General's Office

(a) Not enough pre-trial conferences.

(b) No actions being brought for the seizure of property of convicted drug dealers.

(c) No training introduced for Police Prosecutors.

(d) The Police no longer called to assist prosecutors in the selection of jurors.

Education Department

(a) No truant officers being seen or heard from. Many children not attending school.

Given the complexities of crime and the need for a professionally coordinated approach a proper action plan would be our best strategy. We must urge all citizens to think about how they can assist at the national, community and personal levels in making this integrated crime fighting plan work. The awakening of national consciousness and citizen mobilization will be an integral part of a new crime fighting plan, which include all of our law enforcement agencies and the public service.

It is my humble opinion that there is dire need for a committee headed by yourself and including those cabinet ministers whose portfolios include law enforcement agencies and departments in the public service whose records play an important part in the investigation, detection and prevention of crime.

The inaugural meeting of that committee should be attended also by other selected personnel to include teams from those 0 government departments allied to law enforcement. The Attorney General and the Courts should also be represented.

Recommendations

When the overall crime situation is closely examined every effort must be made to convince the public that concerted actions are taking place and further, that such actions have legitimate, institutionalized, professional backing. An action plan will go a long way in satisfying this public confidence and will help decrease public fear and enhance their feelings of personal security. In the following paragraphs I present an agenda and will briefly discuss each item:

Recruitment and Training

The Force has been experiencing difficulty finding suitable recruits. Many applicants fail the entrance exams. There are options; (a) recruit suitable persons as local constables for special assignments and have such officers further their education on their own time and at their own expense.; (b) recruit a group of foreign personnel on contract as constables for a stipulated period, with annual increments, no promotions and repatriation when contract expires; and (c) encourage those efficient officers to stay on provided they are healthy. They can be used for the on the job training so badly needed.

Crime Statistics, Public Policy and Efficient Records

Law enforcement agencies such as, the F.B.I., the D.E.A., and Scotland Yard thrive on good records. Problems exist with the availability and accessibility of records in certain public service departments. Police computers must be linked to departments such as, Road Traffic, Immigration, National Insurance and the Elections Register.

Ecology of Crime

Identifying high crime areas and implementing prevention strategies. Networking with community and business groups to implement crime watch programs and crime prevention strategies.

Schools and Young People

Security of schools. The failure of some principals to report crime and the lack of support for Police prosecution. Ministry of Education truant officers in communities.

Community Advisory Councils

Each Police Station area should have such a council to provide quick community assistance and consolidation for Police-Community Relations. Use to strengthen Crime Watch Groups. M.Ps should get involved.

Prisons

Prison security - New Providence and a Family Island. Alternatives to incarceration. Electronic equipment for stations.

The Courts

Bail and sentencing, a major problem with the Police. We do not understand how persons charged with serious crimes such as murder, attempted murder and armed robberies are able to get bail so easily.

Plea bargaining. Speedy trials. Court Costs should be introduced. Security of the courts should include electronic surveillance.

Review of Legislation

Fixed Penal ties. Some minor traffic offences not including the process of service needs to be upgraded. Witness Protection. Depositions. Notarise statements.

Discipline

In the Police Force there is a grave need for restoring the discipline we once had, which would enhance efficiency and respect. The thrusts would have to come from those middle management officers. Without discipline efficiency and effectiveness suffers. There have been several instances involving the escape of persons in custody for serious crimes where there was gross neglect due to poor discipline. Some junior officers are very lax in carrying out instructions and supervision is so lacking breaches of security and violations of Force Policy are not even observed until some major incident occurs. In my lectures to classes at the College and on Police Stations I continue to refer to discipline, which in my opinion is a major problem.

Zero Tolerance

It is evident that in spite of instructions from the executive management of the Force the zero tolerance concept of policing is not being fully enforced. In fact I would say it is not being enforced. The enforcement of this concept would most certainly help to restore order, respect for the law of the land and most importantly respect for the Police.

If the public observes a reduction of the lawlessness on our streets, the public would become aware that the Police is very active and would feel safer. The criminal would also observe the change in Police activity and there will be some fear in him about being caught in the act. The zero tolerance concept has worked effectively to reduce crime in many cities, including; New York, Miami, Chicago, Toronto and several other cities around the world. In Nassau and Freeport there were instances when the Police checking vehicles for minor traffic offences detected major crimes and apprehended persons wanted for serious crimes.

In recent weeks a car being chased for speeding was abandoned and the owner was found locked in the trunk. I have tried to motivate the officers in lectures by informing them that the arrests made in the Oklahoma bombing were due to a minor offence being dealt with by a traffic office who observed a car proceed through a school zone above the speed limit, also the arrests made in the bombing of the train in Japan were the result of minor traffic violations being observed by Policemen and enforced.

The commanding officers of the divisions in the Force must regularly monitor the performance of their personnel in the zero tolerance enforcement concept. When the public stop seeing motorcyclists riding dangerously on our streets to our peril; vehicles being driven without number plates; dangerous loads being conveyed on trucks, uncovered loads of garbage littering the streets while being drive to the dump; obstruction caused by buses; illegal parking; speeding and dangerous driving and the scores of other minor offences seen daily they will become aware that our Policemen are active and order is being restored to our society.

When the overall crime situation is closely examined, one recognizes that there is a great need for the general public to be convinced that indeed concerted actions are taking place. The zero tolerance concept is a way of convincing the public.

Credibility

Over the years credibility of the Police has taken a nose dive, at the same time the expectations and demands on the Police have increased to the extent that the Police is finding it difficult to cope with their normal duties of prevention and detection of crime. It is very encouraging that in the area of major crime investigations by the Police have been very effective and significant numbers of persons have been arrested for these crimes. It is a pity that this level of enforcement is not visible in the case of minor offences. The public has difficulty understanding why so many Officers walk pass minor violations and fail to act. Some persons blame the present condition and the crime trend on corruption in the Force. Many who do so on the talk shows would not be prepared to produce any evidence to support their claims. There is a lack of motivation to deal with the minor offences, the lack of intestinal fortitude, family and friendship get involved and the nation suffers.

Public Relations

Community policing has made some inroads towards getting public cooperation with the Police, (which is evident judging from the number of calls being received daily from persons giving information about crime and suspected persons) more needs to be done in areas, such as; publicizing heroic performances by policemen, giving factual information to the public on blatant lies being told about law enforcement officers, responding to claims by talk show hosts, some of whom are considered to be community leaders of corrupt practices and discrimination by law enforcement officers and most importantly crime prevention education.

So many of our residents do things daily that tend to make them targets of criminals. The Police must engage the services of radio media to educate the public on how to conduct themselves during this period of crime. They must be more alert, observant and careful with their property and use all of the available preventative measures and equipment to protect themselves and their properties.

The Police are not placing sufficient emphasis on educating the public. It is a task for the media and the Police. There are so many crimes reported in the daily crime reports that are preventable. In recent weeks I have lectured to church groups on crime prevention and persons expressed amazement at some of the preventable crimes being committed in our country.

The law enforcement executive is professionally crippled if he cannot effectively communicate the strengths and needs of his

Force to the community he serves through relations with the press, radio and television. Instances of significant accomplishments resulting from active cooperation between the public and officers are infinite. Educational campaigns aimed at reducing traffic casualties have been dramatically effective in many countries through the Police and the journalist. Publicity has time after time led directly to the early apprehension of fugitives and wanted persons and to the success of investigations of wide public interests.

Prompt and factual news accounts of accomplishments, whether outstanding or routine which demonstrate determination of purpose and sound professional competence properly emphasize the futility of lawlessness and underscore police dedication to duty. It is one of the virtues of our democratic society that relationship between police and news media is not forever smooth.

On occasion, alert and aggressive newsmen develop sound evidence of abuse of authority, gross dereliction of duty, or outright corruption. Society likely benefits and the Force becomes aware when such corruption is exposed. The large majority, however, of well meaning, honest officers dedicated to fair and effective administration of justice need and receive the encouragement and support of the press. The Police needs it's own hourly radio program once weekly for public relations and crime prevention education.

It is hoped that you will give favourable consideration to the idea of hosting the inaugural meeting suggested earlier in this document, after which we may be able to devise a national plan of action against crime. It would be necessary thereafter for regular meetings to be held jointly by law enforcement agencies to evaluate and improve the plan. Also to communicate regularly with each other in such a forum.

Please be assured of my full cooperation in all matters of mutual interests.

Yours respectfully,

Paul Thompson

APPENDIX 7

Speech on Private Security at the Caribbean Police Commissioners Conference on Paradise Island, 2012

The purpose of security, in its widest sense, is to protect a way of life and for this reason, much time and effort has been devoted throughout the ages to its achievement. It is agreed that the best deterrent against crime and disorder is an efficient and effective police service. Many resort operators and business owners require an effective, efficient and disciplined private security force - one that is well-trained, honest, reliable and responsible.

In our new approach to private security, it should be understood from the outset that the object to be attained is the prevention of crime and the preservation of good order on the properties assigned to private security personnel. To this end, all of those involved in the business of providing private security must direct their efforts.

The enforcement of the customer's policies and regulations must also be a goal. Every effort must be directed towards the security and safety of persons and properties, the preservation of tranquility, and the protection of assets. Every member of the security force must endeavour to distinguish themselves by such vigilance and activity, which would render it impossible for anyone to commit a crime within the confines of the property they are assigned to protect.

In this era of rapidly expanding technology, governmental and private organizations alike require increasingly sophisticated and effective security services to counter both internal and external threats to their personnel, facilities, assets and services. From patrol procedures to alarm systems, from crowd control to investigations and incident response, effective security is a highly visible deterrent to crime and potential problems, such as disorder. It must be understood that effective security services can be delivered only in an atmosphere of training, discipline and re-training.

Only a limited number of security companies provide classroom and on-the-job training constantly for their officers. Some provide handouts to their officers, which contain the basic information regarding their duties at the various locations where they are assigned. These handouts are intended as a form of job training. A book entitled - Basic

Training for Security Officers, written by Paul Thompson, a former Assistant Commissioner of Police and Director of Security at the Atlantis Resort and the Crystal Palace Resort has been well received as an instruction manual as it contains the basic information required to start a security officer's career.

Wemco Security & Collections Ltd is one of the security firms with a profound commitment to training. Wemco executives believe that their training methods will achieve the required standard of performance by their security personnel, which will enhance the reputation for security and safety at the properties where they are assigned to protect. It will also enhance the image of the security company and more persons will look to them for services.

It is my opinion, that the government should play a more active role in the training of security officers. My major concerns for many years are: (a) poor conditions of service for security officers; (b) lack of training; and (c) poor performance. Suggestions have been made to successive governments to consider the following:

1. The Commissioner of Police to be responsible for the registration of security firms.

2. Training of security officers to be conducted at the Police College, at the expense of security firms.

3. Appointment as a security officer to be subject to passing a final exam.

4. Security officers to be considered supplemental police officers.

In the Bahamas, private security is engaged in a price war, which is not beneficial to the industry, the customer or the country. The fees charged for security services are meagre and the type of service rendered in many instances is below what the standard ought to be. Some firms are able to operate at a very low rate of pay and substandard working conditions, which enables them to compete successfully with those firms that try to lift working conditions to a level that would motivate security officers to perform more efficiently and effectively.

Security companies are paying wages as low as $3 per hour with security officers working 12-hour shifts so as to supplement their wages. In many instances there is no training and most importantly no insurance coverage. The result being, that customers get what they are paying for. The result of all this is that the lowly paid security officers are not providing the standard of performance expected by the customer, which in many instances causes persons to lose confidence and respect for those invoked in the industry.

Private security could have a major impact on the war on crime in our country, provided that the government, through the police service, would get involved in the training and certification of security officers. There are many examples of outstanding and courageous performances by security officers, who have been commended by Commissioners of Police. The relationship between the police service and private security is cordial. They assist each other.

At a recent conference sponsored by the Ministry of Tourism and the Royal Bahamas Police Force, it was pointed out that many of our hotels are either without security staff or with grossly inadequate security staff. In many instances the operators of hotels do not give priority to security and safety, considering it to be a non-revenue earner and not that important to the hotel operation.

The double murders of European tourists at a hotel in Bimini and the rape and armed robbery of visitors at a hotel in Cable Beach confirmed that security at both locations was grossly inadequate. The Ministry of Tourism must consider making adequate security a criteria for the licensing of hotels. There must be a suitable qualified person appointed to the Hotel Licensing Authority, who can conduct proper surveys to determine whether security and safety provisions at hotels are adequate.

Security can be a good a career for young people, but those involved must be prepared to train and be trained so as to qualify themselves. Private security firms must improve their selection process and provide decent working conditions for their employees.

In recent years a major effort was made by Byron Rodgers of Maximum Security Company to unite all of the private security firms into an association. He had the full support of the then Commissioner of Police, Paul Farquharson. Meetings were well attended by representatives of security firms operating in The Bahamas. Mr Rodgers had a constitution drafted at his expense, a document listing the aims and objectives of the association and regulations for the administration of the association.

The efforts of Mr. Rodgers and Commissioner Farquharson failed due to the lack of support from the major security firms. The initial meetings discussed issues like training, conditions of service, recruitment standards, pricing, firearms use and closer relations with the police. Such an association is needed in The Bahamas.

Response to award from Trinbagonians in The Bahamas on Occasion of the 50th Anniversary of Trinidad & Tobago's Independence, August 2012

As the government and people of Trinidad & Tobago celebrate half a century of political independence from British colonialism, today even the sharpest critic of Dr. Eric Williams would find it extremely difficult to ignore the tremendous intellectual and political contributions that have inscribed him on history's page as father of the nation.

Three weeks ago the government and people of Jamaica were also occupied in similar celebrations. And Prime Minister Kamla Persad Bissessar was there standing shoulder to shoulder with her Jamaican counterpart, Prime Minister Portia Simpson Miller, to demonstrate that infectious West Indian bond of friendship that binds us as peoples of ONE CARIBBEAN.

I recall the failure of the West Indian Federation, which was buried in the ballot boxes of a Jamaican referendum 51 years ago, when Dr. Eric Williams coined the phrase "one from 10 equals zero". Jamaica and Trinidad & Tobago, the first two to shed the yoke of colonialism, are still tied to Britain's Privy Council as their final appellate court. Our politicians continue with an endless word game about accessing the Caribbean Court of Justice.

This is not a legacy that Eric Williams or Norman Manley would have wanted to perpetuate, but it remains the political burden sustained by politicians of both nations. It confirms what has been said by me before. We can unite in our cricket and music, but not in politics. An independent Trinidad & Tobago owes much to Dr. Eric Williams' vision and commitment. God bless the nation, its government, and its many peoples.

Attending the celebration with Paul Thompson. Sr. were Paul R. Thompson III (grandson), Anthony Blair Moss (grandson), Justyn Coakley (grandson), Andrew Wright (great grandson), and Tracy Blair (daughter).

Commendations

October 28, 1992

Dear Mr Thompson:
I would like to take the opportunity to thank you for your assistance to the Office of the Resident Agent in Charge, US Customs Service, Nassau. On many occasions you have promptly and effectively responded to Customs requests for assistance.

Your conscientious efforts have significantly contributed to the success of the Customs mission. Your dedication and professionalism are truly commendable. Please know that your support is very much appreciated.

Carol Hallett
Commissioner of Customs
Washington DC

August 27, 2010

Certificate of Appreciation awarded to Paul Thompson, Assistant Commissioner of Police (Retired) in recognition of invaluable advisory services to the Central Detective Unit and the Royal Bahamas Police Force

Leon Bethel
Officer in Charge, CDU

By the Queen's Order, the name of Paul Rupert Thompson, detective sergeant of police, was published in the London Gazette on February 6, 1962, as commended for brave conduct. I am charged to record Her Majesty's high appreciation of the service rendered.

May 27, 1970

Dear Mr Thompson:
The splendid assistance afforded by you and other members of the Bahamas Police Force, which resulted in the recovery of a $1,000,000 US Treasury Bill and the arrest of two individuals on May 1 has been brought to my attention. I would like to take this occasion to express to you my appreciation for this fine cooperation.

J. Edgar Hoover,
Director,
Federal Bureau of Investigation

CPSIA information can be obtained at www.ICGtesting.com
Printed in the USA
LVOW10s1200010913

350448LV00002B/6/P